Grasping the Heel of Heaven

Grasping the Heel of Heaven

Liturgy, leadership and ministry in today's church

Edited by

Aidan Platten

CANTERBURY
PRESS
Norwich

First published in 2018 by Canterbury Press
Editorial office
3rd Floor, Invicta House,
108–114 Golden Lane,
London EC1Y 0TG.

Canterbury Press is an imprint of Hymns Ancient & Modern Ltd
(a registered charity)

13A Hellesdon Park Road, Norwich,
Norfolk, NR6 5DR, UK
www.canterburypress.co.uk

978 1 78622 002 8

Typeset by Manila Typesetting Company
Printed and bound in Great Britain by
CPI Group (UK) Ltd

Contents

Change – including everyone

Preface

This book is a very fitting way to honour the ministry of Michael Perham. The subjects within touch those areas of the Church of England's life to which Michael gave so much.

As a liturgist, his legacy will be with the Church for many years to come. Major revision of liturgy is a generational work. It is something that has to be done sensitively, and with much consultation. Often, attempts to achieve such revision founder on the complexities. By his perseverance and imagination, Michael was instrumental in providing the Church with a liturgy which has found a very broad acceptance, and is a rich resource. It has also helped many other parts of the Anglican Communion to shape their own liturgies. Michael would be first to acknowledge that Common Worship was a collaborative work by necessity. But the consistent guiding hand of Michael can be discerned in so much of what is given to the Church. As a dean and a bishop, he showed what can be achieved by liturgy well conducted, and has constantly been concerned to equip people to reach high standards in worship.

But Michael was also someone who contributed to the life of the Church through General Synod. He was a skilful Chair of the Business Committee, which ensured that the conduct of General Synod went as well as it possibly could. Like so much of his ministry it was done modestly and courteously but with determination and persistence. He gave up this work when as he put it he was 'relegated to the Bishops' Bench' but he continued to be someone who would work to bring the best out of the synodical system rather than just complaining about its inadequacies.

He was also persistent and determined in his advocacy of the ordination of women to the priesthood and the episcopate. There are so many men and women who remain grateful to Michael for his unwavering support during times when the obstacles to reaching an agreement seemed insurmountable.

In all this, Michael maintained a very demanding and full life as a diocesan bishop. He cared for his clergy and was attentive to the details of diocesan organization, but having attracted able colleagues, knew when to trust them and let their ministries flourish. He still found the space to accept a number of national responsibilities and civic responsibilities.

In all this what is apparent is that Michael loved the Church, not for its own sake, but because it is called to be the Body of Christ. In serving the Lord Jesus Christ, the incarnate Son of God, nothing less than the best will do, and it was the best that Michael sought to give to the Church, and to help the Church to be.

+Justin Cantuar
Lambeth Palace, London

Introduction: Grasping the Heel of Heaven

AIDAN PLATTEN

Angel voices ever singing
Round thy throne of light,
Angel harps for ever ringing
Rest not day nor night;
Thousands only live to bless thee
And confess thee
Lord of Might.

Thou who art beyond the farthest
Mortal eye can scan,
Can it be that thou regardest
Songs of sinful man?
Can we know that thou art near us,
And wilt hear us?
Yea, we can.

For we know that thou rejoicest
O'er each work of thine;
Thou didst ears and hands and voices
For thy praise design;
Craftsman's art and music's measure
For thy pleasure
All combine.

In thy house, great God, we offer
Of thine own to thee;
And for thine acceptance proffer

All unworthily
Hearts and minds and hands and voices
In our choicest
Psalmody.

Honour, glory, might and merit
Thine shall ever be,
Father, Son and Holy Spirit,
Blessed Trinity.
Of the best which thou has given
Earth and heaven
Render thee.[1]

Angel Voices Ever Singing

Never should a generation pass without the Church questioning both its vocation and whom it is called to serve. Certainly, the last century of British history has seen huge changes and the Church of England has itself contributed to a changing society. The State's response to some of the Church's social work, by implementing a system of benefits for those in need and free health care for all, has challenged the Church in some ways to seek its purpose again. The Church was once a bastion of social reform and the first provider of free education, but the State caught up and took over many elements of its social work. Some will say, then, that the Church in this first quarter of the twenty-first century stands at a crossroads and has decisions to make about which way it should turn. The Church must ask again whom it is to serve and how best it might do that. Francis Pott's great hymn is, in a sense, our anthem for this volume. It reminds the Church that its work is to point people to God and to reflect God's glory and love to the world.

This volume of essays is dedicated to Bishop Michael Perham. Michael's gifts to the Church were immense. As a bishop's chaplain,

1 Francis Pott, 1861, *Hymns Ancient and Modern*.

parish priest, cathedral precentor, dean and diocesan bishop, he believed in the Church as the body of Christ and sought to find ways of nourishing that body by encouraging it in worship and prayer and in examining itself in the light of gospel ideals in its governance.

The title of this volume, 'Grasping the heel of heaven', comes from a chapter of his book *Lively Sacrifice*, which was later re-worked alongside *Liturgy Pastoral and Parochial*, with new material added, to help with the introduction of Common Worship in 2000.[2] 'Grasping the heel of heaven' is a phrase he penned and used and loved. Michael was always worried that both the Church's vision of how worship should be and the accompanying expectation of worshippers as they embark on worship were set too low.

Francis Pott's hymn *Angel Voices* was, in a sense, Michael's anthem too. It offers a picture of heaven, rather like that in Psalm 150, where there are angels singing and playing their instruments, giving glory to God, and affirming that our earthly offering, flawed and imperfect though it might be, is heard and even enjoyed by God. It touches the heart of Michael's ministry. He worked tirelessly to help people engage with God through prayer and worship.

> Worship is to enable us to reach up to grasp the heel of heaven, to glimpse, albeit imperfectly and fleetingly, the life of heaven, to plug in, for a moment, to the worship of the angels and the praises of the saints . . . My worry is not that our worship falls short of this . . . I am not worried that we fail to find ourselves caught up in the holiness around the throne of God every time we share in the liturgy. My worry is that we appear not to expect it ever to happen.[3]

Behind his liturgical work and practice was a constant desire not only to help people engage in a relationship with the Divine, that is to glimpse heaven, but he sought also to change a culture of *surprise* when that occurs, to a culture in which worshippers should *expect*

---

2 Michael Perham, *New Handbook of Pastoral Liturgy* (London: SPCK, 2000).

3 Perham, *Pastoral Liturgy*, pp. 4 and 5.

to glimpse the glory of God and see that the redemptive work of Christ has indeed opened the gates of heaven. The Church in her life and work and worship should help people see the open gates of heaven and see their place in that communion which embraces saints and redeemed sinners.

Michael was clear that while worshippers should expect to meet God in their prayer and celebration, a church that prevented people from entering its orders because of their gender endangered that expectation and so he worked tirelessly for the full inclusion of women in the orders of the Church of England. He was also clear that such changes needed to be brought about in at least three different ways: by careful telling of people's stories, through a rigorous interrogation of the Church's ecclesiology and theology and through sensitive management of the systems and structures of church governance. Glimpsing heaven happens not only in worship but in the encounters we have with each other.

Can We Know That Thou Art Near Us?

People change us – their stories move us.

On a blistering hot day in July 2008, Michael and I set off for Canterbury. I was his driver that day and we arrived at the University of Kent. It was a surreal moment as familiar faces arrived, bishops with their spouses or chaplains or sometimes both, and queued for their room keys, their pectoral crosses glinting in the sun. It was rather like watching grown-ups starting at college all over again.

The Lambeth Conference was not something that Michael had been particularly looking forward to. He and others in Gloucester had enjoyed giving hospitality to bishops of our partner dioceses and beyond, but three weeks or so cooped up in a university with only bishops for company might be a struggle for even the keenest ecclesiast.

Michael was not a huge fan of travelling great distances to exotic parts of the world. He was very keen to support the diocesan links with India and to nurture a new link with Sweden, but being away from home and his regular work didn't greatly excite him.

Collecting Michael at the end of the conference, however, was an eye-opening moment as he had clearly been affected by his experience and changed by it. His already passionate desire for people to find unity with one another in God had connected with the indaba groups at the conference. There he came into contact with two people whose stories were to be important when he returned to Gloucester. One was Mary Gray-Reeves, Bishop of the Diocese of El Camino Real in California, and the other was Gerard Mpango, Bishop of the Diocese of Western Tanganyika.

Together, these three bishops had been affected by their experience of the Lambeth Conference. It was clear to each that, while their opinions on some things might be markedly different, being together and finding themselves united in Christ was moving and energizing. Remembering that both our beginning and our end is in God allows breadth in life.

The stories of both Mary and Gerard brought some change to Michael as, no doubt, his story changed them. On our journey back to Gloucester Michael, though drained by the experience, was enormously fired up about what a relationship between Gloucester, El Camino Real and Western Tanganyika might mean.

There would be moments of real difficulty in setting up the links, but there would be times when heaven touched earth; in the partnership liturgy in Gloucester Cathedral, in the quiet morning office in Michael's chapel, and in times of Lectio Divina.

His desire was that in spite of differences – and quite significant differences – in prayer, worship and study of the scriptures, each could know the nearness of God and a unity with each other through God.

Craftsman's Art and Music's Measure

I spent over four years as Bishop Michael Perham's chaplain in Gloucester. There can hardly be a bishop's chaplain, past or serving, who hasn't found on their tongue at some point Bishop William Walsham-How's words 'we feebly struggle, they in glory shine'. It has become the motto of Mr Slope's successors in the 'Crozier' network of bishops' chaplains. Neither can there be a chaplain who hasn't perceived the privilege that comes with such a ministry, seeing at close hand and sharing in some of the joys and challenges of episcopal ministry.

The City of Gloucester sits, geographically, almost in the centre of the diocese bearing its name. The wilds of Tutshill, Chipping Campden or Wotton-under-Edge are all within about a fifty-minute drive of the episcopal residence, Bishopscourt, and during my tenure I did about half of the driving around the diocese. Many places were too rural for 'Sat-Nav' to be of great help and so journeys out into the farthest reaches would tend to be quite quiet on the way as I concentrated and the Bishop prepared himself for the service; reading through his sermon, ensuring the names of confirmands were firmly lodged in his brain, having a final check on the details of the licence for a new priest and making sure that he was up to speed on what was happening in the parish. In all this, one saw in Michael the 'craftsman's art' as he prepared for countless services, and 'music's measure' as he presided at the liturgy.

The journey home was often more chatty, his post-adrenalin energy keeping a weary chaplain awake as we passed houses with curtains aglow with the flickering of the TV screen. The car was the place in which we could talk about anything. It was the place where the chaplain could feed back the things that only the chaplain can say and where there was an understanding that conversations had in the car, stayed in the car. It was a place of great health. For those who have donned the purple stole in the confessional, the seat belt had a similar effect in ensuring that confidences remained so! It was in the car too where we could reflect on Scripture – whether it be the readings from the offices of the day, or those we would hear at a confirmation or licensing or ordination later. Very regularly Michael would ask what I thought was meant by a particular encounter that Jesus had, or what Peter was really thinking about this or that.

What was almost inevitable was that every visit, every encounter had an effect. Every experience was an experience where something of the Kingdom was discovered. Every place and person left their mark in some way.

In Thy House, Great God, We Offer

Michael's understanding of his vocation throughout his ministry was never narrowly focused on the particular work he was
licensed to. He was a deacon, priest and bishop for the Church
and not just to the cathedral, parish or diocese he happened to be
licensed to at that time.

His work as Secretary to the Doctrine Commission when he
was a curate gave him an inside track on the theological thinking of the Church and how the mechanics of decision-making
worked. As a liturgist he was then in a position to respond to
the needs of worshippers – Michael being more aware of their
needs than perhaps they were themselves – and to do so in ways
that might help communicate the theology and ecclesiology of
the Church. For over forty years, he served in a church that has
evolved at such an astonishing rate that it might be understood
as revolution. It is a revolution that for some is still too slow and
for others leaves them in the midst of a church that they struggle
to recognize.

Through all that, though, what I saw, worked and lived with
was someone whose faith continued to grow deeper daily and
whose commitment to Christ never wavered. His capacity for
hard work far outclassed many and at times he was terrifyingly
focused. It is, in part, that ability to focus that has helped the
Church engage in internal discussions that have interested many
beyond its normal boundaries. Elements of that work brought
with it pain and difficulties that still endure for some and great
joy for others, and the conversations are far from over. Michael
longed for more open and friendly conversations across all the
divisions. He would often quote Gregory of Nazianzus about the
need to be friends with God. If we are true friends of God, we can
learn how to be friends of one another.

Michael's episcopal ring is engraved with *Ut unum sint*, 'That
they may be one'. Taken from the prayer to the Father in John's
Gospel, it was Michael's wish for the Church, and not just for
the Church but for all people. Michael longed for the Church
to be one, but not just with itself. It isn't all about being happy

together, though that would be good. It is about the Church being one with God. 'That they may be one as we are one.'

Jesus' prayer to the Father in John 17 is a prayer that Michael prayed regularly. His daily prayer life, his expectation of meeting God in prayer, and his heart open to God's call on him – these, together with the love and support of Alison and their daughters, are undoubtedly what carried him through an extremely diffi-cult final few months as Bishop of Gloucester and into the early months of retirement. They continued to uphold him in his final months. Michael frequently urged confirmation candidates in the Diocese of Gloucester to 'love the Church, stick with her – even when she drives you up the wall!' Michael lived what he taught.

Michael Perham's story will have changed many of us. It will have changed us in ways that we don't even realize. In his final few months, Michael maintained his work with the University of St Mark and St John in Plymouth, laying foundations for its future; he continued to teach in the Diocese of Salisbury, leading hundreds in days on prayer, and this in the last few weeks and months before his death.

Of the Best That Thou Hast Given

This book is dedicated to, and in thanksgiving for, the ministry of Bishop Michael Perham: an exemplar of the faith, hope and charity that the apostle Paul taught was the vocation of the early church in Corinth, and surely remains so always and everywhere.

In this book, we look at three areas of the Church's vocation in which Michael was particularly interested, and in and over which he exercised some influence. These areas are: the Church's offering of liturgy; the ways in which the Church makes decisions and func-tions at an organizational level; and the ways in which the Church tries to communicate the unconditional love of God for the world. This book does not pretend to solve problems, but instead intends to serve as both a reminder of some of our history and to point forward to ways in which we might keep conversations open.

This volume might seem rather internally focused as we look at liturgy, synodical decision-making and issues of inclusion in the

Church. However, these are all things that those both within and without the Church have heard about and, to the annoyance of some, are actually interested in! Sometimes this is because of news of possible schism and sometimes because of their historical connections with the Church. There is still some corporate memory of the Church within the English people. Beautiful phrasing and cadences of the Prayer Book lie in the memory bank of generations, and so news of seemingly new-fangled prayers worry some. Those who have lived through a time of emancipation will have been pleased with the news of Synod challenging pay-day lenders and pleased to see the pictures of Libby Lane as she became the first woman to be consecrated bishop in the Church of England. These are all signs to those beyond church that something is alive. They serve as reminders to those called to specific ministries within the Church that their church is sacramental in nature; that the things people see the Church doing on the outside tell them something of the nature of the divine working within.

Uncle Lionel (not actually my uncle but the father of a close family friend) had a couple of well-used phrases. 'I'll tell you a story' is the one that continues to resonate. He was a priest and he knew the power of the story. The redemption of the world by Jesus Christ is told primarily in stories; God's wonderful deeds and love are told in stories. From the Prodigal Son, the Wedding at Cana, the feeding of the multitude, all the way to the road to Emmaus – it is stories that communicate the faith and the works of God. This collection of essays is intended to help remind us of some of the recent stories of the Church of England. They tell of a church where much change has happened; too slow for some and too fast for others. They tell of how this church has striven to discern the Holy Spirit and how that discernment is ongoing.

Honour, Glory, Might and Merit Thine Shall Ever Be

Michael Perham played a significant role within the narrative of the past forty years. He loved, served and remained utterly loyal to the Church, which on occasion tested that loyalty. But most of all, till the end of his life, it was his love of his Lord that shone through – honour and glory of that same Lord were the foundation. In the months before he died, Michael knew that this collection was coming together. He was enormously grateful and touched that people might want to contribute to such a volume in thanksgiving for his gifts to the Church.

I am deeply grateful to the contributors, all of whom Michael would count as friends. Each brings to this volume their own particular specialism and passion and each has their own take on those themes which so engaged Michael throughout his ministry. The brief was to write on a particular aspect of Michael's interests from their own discipline and background. What we have in this volume are wonderfully diverse styles and sometimes variant views, which in itself says something about the broad friendships that Michael maintained. However, unity is found as each ultimately points us to hope, and more specifically to hope through the possibility of change. The willingness of the contributors to add to their already considerable workloads says something of the esteem in which Michael was held.

We offer this collection as a reminder of where the Church has come from and how it has worked to bear witness to Jesus Christ. We offer this too as a celebration of what it has achieved and as a reminder of conversations that are still ongoing.

The National Governance of the Church of England: A Brief History

WILLIAM FITTALL

Introduction

How churches are governed is a less interesting subject than what they believe and do. Yet the structures and decision-making processes of any church reflect its beliefs about how God intends the redeemed community of Jesus Christ to be organized here on earth. They also have an impact on its capacity to adapt wisely and effectively in the light of the changing contexts and cultures in which it seeks to proclaim the good news.

There have been many moments in history when arguments about authority, ministry and church order have provoked acute division. While the consequences of many past splits over such issues of faith and order are still with us, the ecumenical movement of the past hundred years has helped ease some of the former soreness and led to a new willingness among Christians to co-operate across denominational boundaries. It has also led to an increased acknowledgement that differences of structure and governance are not wholly, or sometimes even mainly, about underlying differences of theology. History, culture and tradition have all played their part.

Even so, ecclesiology – the study of churches and how they are organized – can never be simply a subset of anthropology, history and sociology to the exclusion of theology. This is as true for the Church of England as for other denominations, despite the fact that the immediate circumstances which triggered the departure of the English Church from the communion of the Roman Church in the 1530s owed more to the politics of the day (in Rome and London) than to theology.

From 1533 to 1920

The years of turbulence

Rather like Brexit, the unexpected break with Rome posed a host of novel and intricate questions to which answers had quickly to be improvised. Previously the English Church had been subject to three sources of law: the canon law of the Roman Church; the common law of England; and statute law made by the Crown in Parliament. Appointments and discipline within the Church had been primarily a matter for the church hierarchy (in many cases involving Rome itself), though the Crown and other important land owners had effective control of some appointments. The two provincial Convocations of Clergy – for York and Canterbury – had had the right to deliberate the conduct of internal church business and the key power of raising taxes from among the clergy.

In order for the Church of England to be able to operate as a free-standing national institution, various gaps had to be plugged. Canon law was retained as a source of authority, with the power to initiate changes to canon law vested in the Convocations. There were, however, two key new provisos: that canons could no longer be made without the royal licence; and they could not be in conflict with the general law of the land.

Appointments previously made by Rome became the prerogative of the Crown. The Convocations survived but they could meet only with the consent of the Sovereign. Subsequently, in 1664 their significance was perceptibly reduced when their power of taxation over bishops and clergy was surrendered to the Crown.

These were all major changes. In addition, while liturgy and doctrine initially remained unchanged in the immediate aftermath of the break with Rome, the influence of Reformation thinking was strong by the middle of the sixteenth century when the Church of England came to develop its own Prayer Book, produce a new framework of doctrine (the Thirty-Nine Articles) and adopt new pastoral practices (notably permission for clergy to marry).

Nevertheless, the Church of England experienced more structural continuity at the Reformation than did those continental churches where the trigger for breaking with Rome had been more avowedly theological. It remained an episcopal church; it retained cathedrals; it continued to be run within two provinces, each with its own metropolitan; ministry continued to be provided by episcopally ordained priests and deacons within dioceses and parishes; church discipline continued to be overseen by ecclesiastical courts; diocesan bishops continued to sit in Parliament. Arguably the biggest governance change was that the new powers of Crown and Parliament gave the laity a much greater say than previously in the running of the Church.

The eighteenth and nineteenth centuries

After the turbulence of the sixteenth and seventeenth centuries – including the brief restoration of Catholicism in the 1550s and the suppression of episcopacy and the Book of Common Prayer through the 1650s – the governance and structures of the Church of England remained largely unchanged throughout the eighteenth century.

The altered balance of power between Crown and Parliament after 1688 and the emergence of the pivotal new role of prime minister from the 1720s did, however, start to have an impact on how decisions affecting the Church[1] were taken. The emergence of an executive formally appointed by the Sovereign but in practice dependent on commanding a majority in the House of Commons meant that legislation affecting the Church required the acquiescence of the prime minister and his cabinet if it was to get through Parliament. Similarly, senior church appointments

---

1 To reduce tedium this chapter will from here on sometimes refer to the Church of England simply as 'the Church', where it is clear from the context that that is what is meant. The Church of England does of course make no claim to be other than a small part of the 'one, holy, Catholic and Apostolic Church'.

increasingly depended on the patronage of the prime minister. By the time that George III abruptly appointed Charles Manners-Sutton as Archbishop of Canterbury in 1805 without taking any advice from his prime minister, William Pitt felt able to protest vehemently that such a step was unconstitutional (though, faced with a fait accompli, he stopped short of resigning).

By the 1830s it was clear that the Church, like many other English institutions, was in serious need of reform to meet the challenges of a society transformed by the appearance of the new, industrial towns and cities of the Midlands and the North. In 1836 Parliament accepted proposals from the government for the establishment of Ecclesiastical Commissioners with powers to redistribute church resources so that ministry could be provided in the new population centres.

Parliament also legislated to curb what had come to be seen as abuses in the Church such as pluralism. One of the more dubious claims to fame of the parish of Saltwood, where I serve as a reader in the Canterbury Diocese, is that its rector from 1812 to 1867, Archdeacon John Croft, lived sufficiently long to be one of the last surviving pluralists. The living to which he was presented by the aforementioned Archbishop Manners-Sutton (his father-in-law) generated a good income in itself but was just one of his port-folio of offices. Together they produced what was, for the time, the colossal annual income of £5,000 (worth around £350,000 today).

The process of reform continued throughout the century. Par-liament agreed to the creation of a number of new dioceses (though on condition that the number of bishops in the House of Lords remained capped at 26). The Commissioners both brought greater order and professionalism to the management of the Church's his-toric assets and channelled significant financial support to support Church growth. In addition the Convocations resumed meeting for business from the middle of the century after more than a cen-tury of quiescence. By the end of the century each had the benefit of input from advisory houses of lay men. In 1903 all four bodies came together to constitute the Representative Church Council, the Church of England's first national assembly (though with only a deliberative role).

These changes were, however, not sufficient to meet the growing conviction, both in the Church and in Parliament, that more far-reaching governance reform was needed to reflect changed circumstances. One consequence of the repeal of the Test and Corporation Acts in 1828 and the passing of the Roman Catholic Relief Act 1829 had been that non-Anglicans were now involved, as MPs, in legislating for the affairs of the Church of England. While for most Anglicans this did not call into question whether the Church of England should remain the established church it did stimulate fresh interest in the idea of spiritual independence from the civil authorities and in the Church having free-standing institutions of governance.

Pressure for change increased as successive governments gave relatively low priority to finding parliamentary time for much-needed new church legislation. This was partly because Parliament was busy legislating to expand the responsibilities of the State and create new public authorities. In some cases the latter were given responsibilities which had previously been exercised only by church institutions. Thus, for example, the General Register Office had been created in 1837 with responsibility for the registration of births, deaths and marriages. From 1870 school boards were created and state-funded primary schools introduced alongside those of the Church. In 1894 new parish councils were created to take over from vestry committees the civil functions of the parish, including the administration of the Poor Law.

This progressive separation of church and state responsibilities made it increasingly anomalous for the Church of England to have no governance bodies of its own at national level save Parliament and the two institutions which, though under significant church influence, were creations of the State – the Ecclesiastical Commissioners and Queen Anne's Bounty (created in 1704 to channel funds to poor clergy).

The Church Assembly

Eventually, the government and Parliament agreed in 1919 to proposals from the Archbishops' Committee on Church and

State[2] for the Church to have its own legislature. This body, the Church Assembly, was a modified version of the Representative Church Council. It was not created at the behest of Parliament but in accordance with a constitution presented to the king by the Convocations of Canterbury and York and laid before Parliament.

What Parliament did in the Church of England Assembly (Powers) Act 1919 was to provide a parliamentary mechanism by which draft primary legislation approved by the new Assembly could be scrutinized for expediency by a Committee of Parliament *especially with relation to the constitutional rights of all His Majesty's subjects*. Then, if approved by each House of Parliament, the legislation could be submitted for royal assent. Such measures, once in force, had the same force and effect as Acts of Parliament. The convention was established that Parliament would no longer legislate for matters within the competence of the new Assembly without the Church's consent.

From 1920 to 1970

Early days

Notwithstanding all the changes that have occurred subsequently, the creation of the Church Assembly in 1920 can fairly be described as the pivotal moment when the governance arrangements of the Church of England assumed a shape that is still recognizable today.[3] The establishment of a national legislature for the Church was part of a wider set of changes designed to make decision-making within the Church more participative.

---

2 The Representative Church Council resolution of 4 July 1913 proposing the creation of the Committee had spoken of the need to 'secure in the relations of Church and State a fuller expression of the spiritual independence of the Church as well as the national recognition of religion'. The Committee reported in 1916.

3 From the outset the Assembly's powers were confined to England because it was also in 1920 that the Welsh dioceses of the Church of England were separated to constitute the new (disestablished) Church in Wales, whose governance structures were modelled on those devised in 1869 for the Church of Ireland.

Each parish was in future to have a Parochial Church Council (PCC). Alongside diocesan conferences, which had a deliberative role, dioceses were, from 1925, required to have a Diocesan Board of Finance (DBF). Each DBF was established as a body corporate and in the course of the twentieth century became increasingly significant in the stewardship of the Church's financial resources and buildings.

Lay membership of the new parish, diocesan and national bodies was open to women as well as men, a fact which would seem unremarkable were it not that it was only in 1970 that for the first time lay women were able to be delegates at the equivalent national body for the Anglican Church in the USA, the General Convention.

The new Assembly's ability to exercise powers over which Parliament had previously had the monopoly gave the Church the capacity to initiate long-overdue changes to the law in order to improve its administration (for example the splendidly titled Ecclesiastical Dilapidations Measure 1923, which dealt with the repair of benefice buildings).

This ability included changing from time to time the powers of the Ecclesiastical Commissioners. Indeed, it was through a measure that the Assembly and Parliament (though not until 1947) agreed to the long-overdue amalgamation of the ecclesiastical commissioners and Queen Anne's Bounty to form the Church Commissioners.

The Church was also for the first time able to take the initiative in seeking to make major changes to its liturgy. In practice this proved to be a harder furrow to plough. The fact that the Convocations retained their previous powers in relation to the canons and continued to meet separately from the Assembly was a complication since significant liturgical change necessitated amendment both of statute law and canon. As a result, complex, parallel processes were necessary in the Assembly and the Convocations. In addition, while Parliament was content not to initiate legislation affecting the internal life of the Church of England, it quickly showed itself suspicious of any attempt by the new legislature to make changes to the liturgy which might be seen as shifting the Church's traditional centre of gravity and thus altering its perceived character.

In 1927 and 1928 the House of Commons rejected draft Prayer Book Measures, essentially on the grounds that they might legitimize certain Catholic beliefs and devotions which, it was argued, had been abandoned at the Reformation. These votes occurred notwithstanding favourable reports from the Ecclesiastical Committee (and, in 1927, a favourable vote in the House of Lords) and the fact that the new Prayer Book was intended to be an alternative to, rather than a replacement for, the Book of Common Prayer, which parishes could choose to use if they wished.

Rather remarkably given their usual deference to law, bishops decided in 1929 to publish the rejected Prayer Book as an unauthorized text and asserted that its use in the present 'emergency' would be regarded as being in accordance with the mind of the Church. This unsatisfactory legal situation was only finally remedied when Parliament agreed in 1965 proposals from the Assembly for a series of experimental liturgies that paved the way for what eventually became (in 2000) Common Worship, an authorized alternative to the Book of Common Prayer.

Constraints

There were at least three other respects in which the limitations of the new national governance arrangements became increasingly apparent over time.

One, as already noted, was that the separate operation of the Convocations and the Assembly meant that processes were cumbersome and, for bishops and clergy expected to attend both bodies, time-consuming. The fact that the Assembly had some 750 members also made it a difficult body in which to participate.

The second was that the breadth of membership of the Assembly and the lack of an executive meant that securing the necessary degree of support for any legislative changes that might affect vested interests was time-consuming, if not impossible. For example, anything touching on the rights that the clergy enjoyed under parson's freehold, including the right to stay in office until death, could not pass without sufficient support from the clergy members of the Assembly.

The third factor – the existence of well-established Anglican voluntary societies – was perhaps the most significant complication for those who had invested great hopes in the potential of the new Assembly and its associated committees, boards and councils to take an overview of the needs of the Church. It was also the complication least susceptible of remedy given that, for many, the diversity of voluntary societies was one of the Church of England's strengths.

During the centuries in which the Church had lacked national institutions of its own those who had wanted to get something new started had had no option but to establish free-standing voluntary societies with their own bespoke governance arrangements. The impeccable credentials of these societies were generally secured by inviting archbishops and/or other senior bishops to bestow their patronage. Thus the Society for the Promotion of Christian Knowledge, the Society for the Propagation of the Gospel, the Church Missionary Society, the National Society (for the promotion of Church schools and Christian education), Hymns Ancient and Modern and many others had become significant parts of the ecology of the Church of England long before the arrival of the Church Assembly.

Other societies – such as the Church Pastoral Aid Society and the Society of the Holy Cross – avowedly carried the banner for particular flavours of churchmanship and were therefore by their nature necessarily at one remove from the Church's formal structures. But societies such as SPCK and the National Society had long been undertaking work that would, as in other churches, have been undertaken under the auspices of the relevant national governing bodies, had such existed.

The theological colleges were a category of complexity in their own right. Created with the support of individual bishops in the nineteenth century when Oxford and Cambridge lost their monopoly of clerical education, each was independent and had its own governance arrangements. While aspiring to train ordinands who would serve across the country, they each occupied a distinctive position in the churchmanship spectrum of the Church of England. As the need for national standards and policies became evident the bishops[4] had agreed to form a national committee, which came into existence in 1913 to oversee theological education.

Thus in relation to at least four major areas of church life – home and overseas mission, church schools, theological education and hymnody – the Assembly found that others had and wished to retain the lead role as well as the resources. The Assembly might hold debates and establish boards, councils and committees of its own to act as ginger groups and promote good practice. But it lacked some of the key levers, risked duplicating work being undertaken elsewhere and faced strong vested interests if ever it was minded to propose changes that the existing societies opposed.

These tensions were never satisfactorily resolved in the lifetime of the Assembly and in some respects continue down to the present day, though they have been significantly mitigated in the course of time. The establishment of a single Chief Education Officer post and lead bishop for education in the mid-1970s, the establishment of Partnership for World Mission as a forum for all the Anglican mission agencies and representatives of the General Synod in 1978 and the creation of a Ministry Council less than a decade ago have all helped.

A *new beginning*

The decision of Archbishop Fisher to make canon law reform a major priority for his primacy (1945–61) cruelly exposed the division of responsibilities between the Convocations and the Church Assembly and the illogicality of involving bishops, clergy and laity in considering draft measures but only bishops and clergy in considering draft canons. The House of Laity was conceded an

---

4 The diocesan bishops of the Church of England were already meeting annually (and privately) at Lambeth by 1874; see Edward Carpenter, *Cantuar: The Archbishops in Their Office* (London: Mowbray, 1997). These meetings had no formal status or governance role.

informal advisory role but the processes were cumbersome and the underlying problem remained.

The process of preparing for a further major overhaul of church governance took many years but eventually the Synodical Government Measure 1969 was agreed. As in 1920, the changes were not confined to the national level. Deanery and diocesan synods were created as well as a General Synod. The latter inherited the powers of the Church Assembly and most of those of the Convocations.

The members of the new deanery synods were entrusted with the responsibility of electing the lay members of General Synod. The total size of the new body was smaller than that of the Church Assembly (under 600 rather than nearly 750) and was reduced further over time – to around 470 voting members in 2005.

From 1970 to the Present

From the old to the new

The General Synod met for the first time on 4 November 1970. For the opening of the Church Assembly in 1920 its Supreme Governor, King George V, had sent a telegram (from Newmarket). On this occasion the Queen attended both the inaugural service in Westminster Abbey and the subsequent start of Synod proceedings in Church House. She has subsequently attended each of the quinquennial inaugurations[5] of the new Synod.

As in 1920 there was a strong sense that a new chapter was beginning in the life of the Church of England. Moreover, the context was changing rapidly. Post Vatican II, relations with the Roman Catholic Church were thawing. There seemed to be a real possibility of reunion with the Methodist Church. A commission under Professor Owen Chadwick had just examined relations between

---

5 Each Synod is constituted for five years, unless dissolved earlier by the Sovereign (see Church of England Convocations Act 1966 and the Synodical Government Measure 1969).

Church and State. The movement for women's ordination, though opposed by many, was gaining strength.

In addition, the Church was starting to have to grapple with the long-term consequences of numerical decline, sharpened by the impact of rising inflation. The need for pastoral reorganization was becoming more acute. Clergy freehold, while cherished by many, was increasingly seen by others as anachronistic. The responsibility for maintaining so many listed buildings, especially in small rural communities, was becoming ever more onerous.

The Church Commissioners were managing the Church's historic resources with conspicuous success but the old arrangements whereby incumbents remained responsible for managing the endowments and glebe of their benefice reflected the realities of an earlier age. And, despite the good stewardship, parishioners were being faced with the need to remedy historically very low levels of giving to support their parish church (estimated at less than 1% of an individual's income in 1978 when the Synod approved a national target of 5%).

The newly created Synod worked hard, in its early years meeting for three groups of sessions of three to five days each February, July and November. In between time legislative committees undertook the more detailed work of revising draft legislation. The result was a number of landmark decisions[6] in the first decade of the Synod's life, including:

- The first amending canon to be made by the Synod (B15A, in July 1972), which legitimized the administration of Holy Communion to communicant members of other Christian churches.
- The Church of England Worship and Doctrine Measure 1974, which gave the Synod power, by canon, to make provision for worship, including for the authorization and use of forms of service, but so that the forms of service contained in the Book of Common Prayer had to continue to be available for use This

---

6 As in the Church Assembly, most decisions in the Synod are taken by simple majority vote but, if a vote by houses is called, approval requires majorities in each of the Houses of Bishops, Clergy and Laity. And some categories of legislation require two-thirds majorities in each house at final approval.

meant that parliamentary consent was no longer needed in these areas, unless it was desired to remove authorization for Book of Common Prayer services.

- Agreement with the government in 1976 on the creation of a Crown Appointments (subsequently renamed Nominations) Commission for the appointment of diocesan bishops. While, until 2007, the prime minister chose to retain the discretion to pick either of the two names submitted by the Commission or to ask it for more names, the choice of eligible candidates now rested with a Commission of the Synod. This change, along with the Worship and Doctrine Measure, drew the teeth of most of the remaining concern in the Synod about Church–State relations.
- Legislation in 1975 introducing mandatory retirement ages from clerical office for future appointments. Legislation permitting the removal of incumbents in the case of pastoral breakdown with their congregations was also passed in 1977, though with provisions that made it, on cost grounds, all but unusable.
- The Endowment and Glebe Measure 1976, which transferred all benefice assets, save the church building, churchyard and parsonage, to the Diocesan Board of Finance. Thus the DBFs were able to bring a more professional approach to the management of the historic assets of incumbents.
- A vote in 1975 asserting that there were 'no fundamental objections' to the ordination of women to the priesthood.

Ecumenism was the area where change proved much more difficult than had seemed possible in 1970. The Synod's decision in 1972 not to give the requisite 75% majority for the Anglican–Methodist unity scheme effectively marked the end of realistic attempts to secure institutional reunion between the Church of England and other churches in any reasonably foreseeable future. That said, and notwithstanding tensions with the Roman Catholics and Orthodox over the ordination of women, practical co-operation between the main Christian traditions continued to grow, with the full encouragement of the Synod, which itself came to include ecumenical observers with the right to speak in its debates.

1992 *and the aftermath*

Through most of the 1980s two dramas were gradually unfolding, one very publicly and one largely beneath the surface. Both were to have a major impact on the Church of England and, by coincidence, both came to a climax in 1992.

One was the debate over the ordination of women, which has been extensively chronicled elsewhere (including in this book). While the decision of the Synod on 11 November to approve the necessary legislation had no direct impact on the governance structures of the Church, it had two important indirect impacts.

Over the following decade, 441 priests left the ministry of the Church of England, predominantly from the Catholic wing of the Church. While the Synod continued to include all shades of opinion from within the Church, including a significant representation of those Catholics and Evangelicals opposed to women's ordination, the churchmanship balance of the Church and the Synod was never quite the same again.

Once the ordination of women as priests began in 1994, the House of Clergy, like the House of Laity (though not till 2015 the House of Bishops), became mixed gender. As a result, over time the gender balance in the Synod changed significantly. The election in 1995 of the first woman to be chair of the House of Laity was followed by the appointment of the first woman priest to chair the Business Committee of the Synod in 2006 and the first election of a female prolocutor (Chair of a House of Convocation) in 2010.

The other drama, unknown to most until a front page *Financial Times* article on 11 July 1992, was the growing agony that the Church Commissioners had been enduring throughout the 1980s in trying to generate sufficient income to meet their commitments to supporting the Church's ministry.

As late as the 1960s, the Commissioners had funded the majority of parish ministry costs. Over the succeeding years this proportion had gradually decreased, leaving dioceses having to levy more from parishes. They in turn had had to ask church members to give more. Even so, the Commissioners continued not only to fund the stipends of bishops and most cathedral clergy, but also to make a significant contribution to diocesan stipend funds and to meet all clergy pension costs.

Eventually the latter proved to be the straw that broke the camel's back. The Commissioners had acquiesced in a Synod decision in 1980 to mandate a substantial enhancement of clergy pension benefits. In doing so they had not properly weighed the long-term impact on their liabilities of what continued to be a non-contributory scheme. Increasingly they came to prioritize income generation at the expense of the long-term value of the fund and to allow themselves to engage in speculative property development. The property crash of the early 1990s hit the Commissioners hard. The *Financial Times* estimated that they had lost £500m. This was later revised to £800m.

The post-mortem ordered by Archbishop George Carey revealed serious governance weaknesses within the Commissioners and paved the way for a series of reforms effected by two pieces of legislation:

- The Pensions Measure 1997 restricted the liability of the Commissioners for clergy pensions to those earned up to the end of 1997 and entitled them to use capital, as necessary, to meet that liability. A new scheme from 1998 was to be funded by way of diocesan contributions into a fund managed by the Pensions Board (which had previously administered the clergy pension scheme but not managed the investments).
- The National Institutions Measure 1998 created a new body corporate, the Archbishops' Council, to which certain Commissioner functions were transferred, in particular responsibility for policy on clergy stipends and pensions and on the distribution of commissioner-generated funds to the dioceses. The legislation made it possible for joint employment arrangements to be established across the Church's national institutions. It also revamped the governance of the Commissioners by reducing their Board of Governors from 95 members to 27 and creating an Audit Committee with the right to escalate concerns to the six state commissioners (the prime minister and five other state office holders).

The creation of the new Council had been proposed in 1995 in *Working as One Body,* an Archbishops' Commission chaired by Bishop Michael Turnbull to 'review the central policy-making and resource-direction machinery of the Church of England'. The Commission had recommended that the Council take over all the Church Commissioners' responsibilities save the management of the Church's historic assets. Although, in the event the legislation was somewhat less far reaching,[7] the narrowing of the Commissioners' responsibilities and the creation of the Council marked a significant reshaping of the national governance of the Church. The Council largely subsumed the responsibilities of the old Synod Standing and Policy Committees (which disappeared) and became the successor body to the Central Board of Finance, which was subsequently wound up.[8]

The new arrangements gradually settled down and there has been no perceptible appetite since then for further major structural change.[9] The Council has met the need for the Church to have a national executive committee with the ability to take an overview of national church business and initiate proposals for change in the light of such strategic vision as the House of Bishops may from time to time set. The Council is accountable in specific ways to the Synod (for example through having to submit its budget for synodical approval), while being a body corporate and registered charity in its own right.

The Commissioners' more focused remit and revised governance arrangements have helped it focus with great success on

---

7 The Commissioners retained responsibility for dealing with appeals against pastoral reorganization schemes and the closure of church buildings. They also continued to run a national payroll bureau for the clergy, hence the tendency of clergy to say that they are 'paid by the Commissioners' though it is in fact each diocese that has the funding responsibility for clergy stipends as well as, under common tenure, responsibility for its parish clergy's terms of service.

8 The CBF had been established as a body corporate as far back as 1914 to hold funds and act as the employer of staff working for the central committees of the Church and subsequently the Assembly and Synod.

9 Even proposals for a relatively limited change which would have abolished various boards and councils (formerly sub-committees of the Archbishops' Council) were dropped in 2009 in the face of opposition in Synod.

its key task of managing the historic endowment effectively. The Pensions Board, with its important responsibilities for managing pension schemes and providing retirement housing for clergy, has no longer had to operate in a semi-dependent relationship to the Commissioners.[10] In addition, the staff of each of the national church institutions, including the archbishops' staff at Lambeth and Bishopthorpe, are now jointly employed and on common terms of service. Common service functions exist, including for HR, finance, communications and legal services.

Some Concluding Thoughts

If a church's governance structures reflect its theology and have an important influence on its effectiveness and adaptability, what can be deduced from the way in which the Church of England is now governed?

First, it remains a church which seeks to hold in creative tension a high view both of the particular role of bishops as guardians of faith, order and liturgy and of the role of the laity in the life, ministry and governance of the Church. The Church of England remains an episcopal church where bishops have a responsibility to lead and govern. Yet ever since the 1530s lay people have exercised a much greater role in church governance than is even now permitted within the Roman Catholic or Orthodox Churches. The mechanisms by which that role has been exercised have changed greatly down the centuries. But it has been a constant.

Second, the Church of England continues to be an institution and an organism rather than an organization. Though by law established, it has many of the characteristics of the rest of the voluntary and community sectors, not least in having an ambiguous attitude towards leadership. In addition, the complexity and

---

10 Indeed, the Commissioners had come near to absorbing the Pensions Board in the mid-1980s, a seriously misconceived proposal that was defeated in the Synod, despite the support of the then Standing Committee, largely because of a speech from the then Synod member, Mr Frank Field MP.

diversity of structures, with a myriad of legal entities at parochial, diocesan and national level and in the Anglican voluntary societies, means that there are few levers of executive power. Leadership depends on influence, persuasion, the building of coalitions and the winning of hearts and minds.

Third, the Church of England's structures and its rootedness in communities give it a low centre of gravity. This is both strength and weakness. Its ability to evolve gradually in the light of changing circumstances has given it great resilience. And the need for a high level of consent for major changes (such as women's ordination) has helped both to avert rash decisions and to put a premium on finding ways to accommodate rather than exclude minorities.

Nevertheless, the Church of England has not found it easy to diagnose and respond purposefully to the reasons for more than a century of gradual decline. And, as the 1830s illustrated, at times when society is changing fast something more dynamic than slow, institutional evolution can be required. The 'renewal and reform' process which is being championed by the archbishops and supported by the Synod is a notable attempt to deliver change more quickly and focus on growth more sharply than previously.

Finally, at the national level, much turns now on the quality of relationship between the Synod, the Archbishops' Council[11] and the House of Bishops and on how the relationship is tended by those who are on more than one of those bodies. Without careful tending each body can look with some suspicion and/or frustration at the other. That is why it helps when, among the diocesan bishops and the suffragans elected to the House and Synod, there are some who have had experience of the Synod before becoming bishops.

Michael Perham was a notable case in point. With a short break in 1992–93 he served continuously on the Synod for nearly 25 years from 1989, first as a parish priest, then as a cathedral dean and finally as a diocesan bishop. He chaired its Business Committee, was a founder member of the Archbishops' Council, served on

---

11 And on particular issues there is also a need for close working between the Council, the Commissioners and the Pensions Board. The First Estates Commissioner is one of the 19 members of the Council.

the House of Bishops' Standing Committee and did much else besides. In particular, he played a leading role in helping reframe the pattern of national episcopal meetings so that meetings of the (synodical) House, of the wider College of Bishops and of diocesan bishops each had their distinctive character and purpose.

He was not someone who sought to contribute by saying the most but by intervening quietly and tellingly at the right moment (his intervention in the Synod debate on clergy vesture in July 2014 is one such example). Above all he was someone who, while rooted in his own churchmanship and secure in his calling as priest and bishop, sought to bring to the national governance bodies of the Church a commitment to the Church of England in all its rich diversity.

Acknowledgements and Bibliography

This chapter is a distillation of knowledge gathered over many years from a wide variety of sources. I am grateful to my predecessor Sir Philip Mawer, to Dr Colin Podmore and to Mr Stephen Slack for checking it for error and offering some helpful suggestions.

Colin Podmore's book *Aspects of Anglican Identity* (London: Church House Publishing, 2005) remains a key text. Chapter seven sets out the history and principles of synodical government.

Martin Davie's *A Guide to the Church of England* (London: Mowbray, 2008) is a useful reference work.

For the thinking lying behind the establishment of the Church Assembly, the *Report of the Archbishops' Committee on Church and State* (London: SPCK, 1917) remains the definitive work. Chapter two also contains an interesting historical survey back to the early medieval period.

Owen Chadwick's magisterial work in two volumes, *The Victorian Church* (London: SCM Press, 1966 and 1970), is illuminating on the nineteenth-century reforms.

2

Bishops, Laity and Synods[1]

MARK CHAPMAN

The Problem of Church Government

The twentieth century has seen a significant number of changes in the governance of the Church of England. These eventually led to the creation of the General Synod in 1970 with its three houses, which do not always see eye to eye. This was further complicated by the establishment of the Archbishops' Council in 1999, as a second executive body alongside the House of Bishops. Steering one's way through the complex Standing Orders and procedures requires an eye for detail which is probably best combined with a sense of the ridiculous. General Synod is undoubtedly an acquired taste. I am not sure whether I was very suitable, but I was persuaded to stand for General Synod in 2010 by a former student who thought it could do with a historian's contribution. My maiden speech in February 2011 reflected on the historical background to the ARCIC report on Mary, and it is probably the only time that Dr Pusey's book on the Immaculate Conception has ever been mentioned on the floor of Synod. It is also highly unlikely that anybody else ever spoke about menstruation in a maiden speech. The debate in which I spoke was chaired by Michael Perham with a wit and a charm that made him one of the best synodical performers during

---

1 This is an expanded and modified version of a lecture delivered at a conference organized by Affirming Catholicism entitled 'Episcopally Led, Synodically Governed', which took place on 24 November 2012 at St Maryle-Bow Church, London. It took place four days after the rejection by the House of Laity in the General Synod of the measure that would have allowed the ordination of women as bishops. An earlier version was published as 'Does the Church of England have a Theology of General Synod?', *Journal of Anglican Studies* 11 (2013), pp. 15–31.

his long time of service. I began my speech by pointing out that the date of the debate was the commemoration of the execution of one of his illustrious predecessors, John Hooper in 1555. 'Ecumenism', I said, 'has come a very long way, so for that we can always give thanks', to which Bishop Michael responded 'I do!'[2] What is often a tense and highly politicized atmosphere requires a lightness of touch to help refocus on the underlying unity of purpose.

But often, there is a degree of suspicion between the different houses and different bodies in the Church that makes such a lightness difficult to find. General Synod is a body that can take itself very seriously, and undoubtedly there are many, not least in the House of Bishops, who might prefer a somewhat more streamlined and managerial method of running the Church, which was perhaps in the mind of those who created the Archbishops' Council. In thinking about the distinctive polity of the Church of England it is always worth reflecting on the experience of other churches. For instance, in 1867 George Talbot (1816–86), the somewhat eccentric English Roman Catholic convert who served as papal chamberlain and who was the (frequently distorting) eyes and ears in Rome of the English Catholic Community, wrote a letter to Henry Manning asking: 'What is the province of the laity?' His answer was given partly in response to Newman, who had published his thoughts on consulting the faithful in matters of doctrine in 1859.[3] Talbot's response to Newman, whom he regarded as a 'wound inflicted on the Catholic Church' and 'the most dangerous man in England', was simple and direct and displayed something of his aristocratic background: the province of the laity, he claimed, was 'To hunt, to shoot, to entertain. These matters they understand, but to meddle with ecclesiastical

---

2 Debate on ARCIC Report: 'Mary: Grace and Hope in Christ' in *Report of Proceedings of General Synod, February Group of Sessions* (2011), 42: 1, GS1818, pp. 196–219 (203–4) at: https://www.churchofengland.org/media/1240726/feb%202011%20consolidated%20with%20index.pdf (accessed 20 February 2017).

3 On the context and fallout of Newman's article see Douglas Woodruff's introduction in Lord Acton, *Essays on Church and State* (London: Hollis and Carter, 1952), esp. pp. 21–3.

matters they have no right at all.'[4] Such an estimation of the laity was something repeated by other prominent English Roman Catholics in the nineteenth century, including the future Cardinal Nicholas Wiseman, at the time titular Bishop of Melipotamus and responsible for the London District, in his pamphlet, Words of Peace and Justice.[5] This polemic was written in the context of the controversy over the (unsuccessful) attempt to establish diplomatic relations with Rome in 1848. Against the wishes of Wiseman, but supported by the Tablet, a meeting had been convened at Freemason's Hall to draft a memorial to Pope Pius IX, which claimed to be in the name of 'English Catholics' and which opposed the normalization of relations. Anxious about upsetting the delicate situation, Wiseman spoke of the 'influx into ecclesiastical and spiritual affairs of principles belonging to temporal and social interests'. He sought a 'well-drawn boundary line'[6] between clergy and laity, so that the Church would be governed by those 'whom the Church has trained, and God has anointed for this purpose'. Like Samuel they had been 'chosen to govern God's people'. Although it was clear that the Church often sought the 'zealous co-operation', 'social influence', 'brilliant talents', 'weighty name' and 'abundant means' of the laity, it was nevertheless the case that 'the direction, the rule, belongs to us'. In short, he concluded: 'We will always gladly see you working with us, but we cannot permit you to lead, where religious interests are concerned.'[7] The clergy, and especially the bishops, and the laity had quite distinct spheres.

---

4 Letter from Talbot to Manning, 25 April 1867, cited in E. S. Purcell, Life of Cardinal Manning, Archbishop of Westminster, 2 vols (London: Macmillan, 1896), II, p. 318.

5 Words of Peace and Justice: Addressed to the Catholic Clergy and Laity of the London District, on the Subject of Diplomatic Relations with the Holy See (London: Dolman, 1848). On this, see James P. Flint, Great Britain and the Holy See: The Diplomatic Relations Question, 1846–1852 (Washington DC: Catholic University of America Press, 2003), ch. 4; Saho Matsumoto-Best, Britain and the Papacy in the Age of Revolution, 1846–1851 (Woodbridge: Royal Historical Society, 2003); Wilfrid Ward, The Life and Times of Cardinal Wiseman (London: Longmans, 1912), 2 vols, I, ch. 16.

6 Words of Peace and Justice, p. 15.

7 Words of Peace and Justice, p. 16.

Such an attitude towards the laity has been something shared by some who have occupied important roles within the Church of England. For instance, John Hooper, Bishop of Gloucester, whom I have already mentioned as one of the martyrs of the Reformation, did not have a high view of the laity. He called the people 'that many-headed monster' which, because of its ignorance, was 'fascinated by the inveiglements of the bishops, and the malice and impiety of the mass-priests'.[8] The people, he felt, were ill-educated and superstitious, and deserved to have little say in the running of the Church.

However much sympathy there might be for such judgements about the role of the laity in church government, there are very few Anglicans who would seek to deny the laity a say in the governance of the Church. There can be very practical reasons for this. In a time when the financial burdens of the Church increasingly fall on the active laity, at least in England, there is a sense in which the principle of no taxation without representation needs to be taken seriously. Just as the origin of the two houses of Convocation (the bishops and the clergy) derived from the need for medieval kings to gain the consent of the clergy for taxation,[9] so the representation of the laity makes sense on purely pragmatic terms. It is interesting to note that despite his High Church inclinations, Bishop Robert Gray of Cape Town, who was one of the pioneers of synodical government in the Anglican Communion, established a House of Laity in the Province of South Africa from the very beginning on such grounds: the Church could not be governed without the consent of the laity who were expected to pay for it. The laity were included in the synod, which was formally set up in 1876, according to Peter Hinchliff, 'not as a result of theological or historical justification, but because they

---

8 Letter from Hooper to Bullinger, 5 February 1550, in *Original Letters Relative to the English Reformation: Written During the Reigns of King Henry VIII, King Edward VI, and Queen Mary: Chiefly from the Archives of Zurich*, ed. Hastings Robinson, 2 vols (Cambridge: Cambridge University Press for the Parker Society, 1846–47) I, 76.

9 See Eric Kemp, *Counsel and Consent: Aspects of the Government of the Church as Exemplified in the History of the English Provincial Synods* (London: SPCK, 1961), esp. pp. 63–142.

possessed the money and power which was needed and because by the nineteenth century a purely clerical gathering would have been not merely unthinkable but unworkable'.[10]

Synods and the Problem of Division

This example from South Africa indicates something crucial about the nature and theology of synods. While much of the literature tends to assume that they are rather grand assemblies whose debates and discussions are geared towards the clarification and articulation of important matters of doctrine and order, they are frequently, at least in origin, very worldly councils. Although Convocations acquired the rights to create canons through the Middle Ages, they spent the bulk of their time discussing the very worldly aspects of church affairs.[11] And often they provided a check on the power and claims of the monarch towards absolute sovereignty over matters both temporal and spiritual. Perhaps because of these very worldly concerns, there has been remarkably little discussion of the theology of synods in the Church of England. Although there have recently been some detailed discussions of the so-called 'conciliar movement' of the Middle Ages,[12] there has been remarkably little theological analysis of our domestic synods, either through history or today.[13] The last full-scale account of synodical history was Eric Kemp's comprehensive Bampton

---

10 Peter Hinchliff, 'Laymen in Synod: An Aspect of the Beginnings of Synodical Government in South Africa', in *Studies in Church History, Volume 7: Councils and Assemblies*, ed. G. J. Cuming and Derek Baker (Cambridge: Cambridge University Press, 1971), pp. 321–7, here p. 327.

11 Kemp, *Counsel and Consent*, pp. 65–86.

12 Francis Oakley, *The Conciliarist Tradition: Constitutionalism in the Catholic Church, 1300–1870* (Oxford: Oxford University Press, 2003); and Paul Valliere, *Conciliarism: A History of Decision-Making in the Church* (Cambridge: Cambridge University Press, 2012).

13 See Kemp, Counsel and Consent, esp. pp. 87–112. See also the 1902 Report: *The Position of the Laity in the Church being the Joint Committee of the Convocation of Canterbury (1902)*, reprint with an introduction by Norman Sykes (Westminster: Church Information Board, 1952).

Lectures of 1960, which offer a thoroughgoing analysis, legal, theological and financial, of the development of Convocation and later of the House of Laity in the Church Assembly, the forerunner of General Synod. Nevertheless, even when synods are discussing such worldly matters as parochial fees, it remains important to think through the theology of the synodical system. The problem, however – and this is something that has been blindingly obvious in recent years – is that they do not seem very theological. Instead they are messy, full of conflict and very political. Often they do not appear to be possessed of the great Christian virtues of faith, hope and love at all. And furthermore they seldom embody anything more than a modicum of unity or consensus.

The Church of England has embraced a system of church government characterized by conflict, compromises and sometimes downright hostility between the factions. This has become apparent ever since the revival of an active Convocation from the middle of the nineteenth century and the creation of the Church Assembly in 1919. When the authority to make its own decisions was returned to the Church following the long dominion of Parliament after that body had long ceased to be a purely Anglican institution, the horse-trading and political wheeling and dealing did not evaporate. What emerged was a system established not on the fact that people agree; instead it quickly became that place where people who disagreed with one another came together to try to make decisions. Synods were necessary not because of any spurious comprehensiveness or unity-in-diversity, but precisely because of the disunity of the Church. This means that it is crucial to bear in mind from the outset that any theology of synodical government is always going to be a political theology: it will be about putting things into practice in a society which is not perfect and which is made up of people with very different ideas of what constitutes truth. It requires what Ephraim Radner has recently called 'eristology', or the study of Christian divisions in their relation to political power.[14]

From my experience, the current General Synod through two Archbishops of Canterbury has not been a particularly happy place;

---

14 Ephraim Radner, *A Brutal Unity: The Spiritual Politics of the Christian Church* (Waco TX: Baylor University Press, 2012), p. 4.

it is highly politicized, and its debates, at least in relation to controversial ecclesiastical matters, so often lack the qualities of listening and learning. Both women bishops and, most recently, issues in sexuality offer good examples. To understand Synod requires a special form of political theology. After all, synods claim to be about discerning the will of God for the Church, which is inevitably a theological act. But because the Church is made up of those odd mixtures of saint and sinner that we call human beings, any form of church government, from the most authoritarian to the most democratic, is always deeply political. Indeed all politics, whether in the Church or in the State or in the parish council, is about power, authority and legitimacy. And, of course, in a strange country like the United Kingdom, where the monarch is still anointed by the Church, the boundaries between Church and State are sometimes rather fluid.

A Theology of Synods

So where are we to start with a theology of synodality? To many people the obvious answer would be in the doctrine of the Triune God. But if synods are founded on conflict and the institutionalization of disagreement (just like parliaments) then it seems to me to be somewhat disingenuous to suggest that the starting point for the theology of synodical government should rest in the doctrine of the Trinity, which, with rare exceptions, has seldom been used to explain conflict, disunity and division. As the political theologian David Nicholls once noted: 'We are urged to think of God as a "society". But what kind of society or community? A good society, undoubtedly. But what is a good society like? What degree of unity is appropriate to a human social group?'[15] His answer was far from straightforward: conflict and division seemed central to human growth and flourishing, a feature he even located in the tensions between Father and Son in the Godhead.[16]

---

15 David Nicholls, 'Trinity and Conflict', *Theology* XCVI (1993), pp. 19–27, here p. 19.

16 See my essay, 'The Social Doctrine of the Trinity: Some Problems', *Anglican Theological Review* 83:2 (2001), pp. 239–54.

Such reservations about the appropriateness of the doctrine of the Trinity in grounding human political communities, however, are rare. Instead it has become a commonplace in church reports and much of the rest of theological literature, including nearly all writing on mission especially after David Bosch's seminal work *Transforming Mission*,[17] that somehow all the Church needs to do is simply to model itself on the harmony and relationality of some imagined Trinity. Father, Son and Holy Spirit offer and receive love to and from one another in a relationship of perfect reciprocity or mutual indwelling. Divine dances and inclusive embraces have become the new orthodoxy in theology.[18] This means that what little theological reflection there has been on the nature of the structures of the General Synod and of the more local synods of the Church of England has simply assumed that somehow the obvious place to start theological reflection on church government should be the doctrine of the Trinity. For instance, in the 1997 Report *Synodical Government in the Church of England*,[19] which remains the most extensive discussion of the nature of the General Synod,[20] the brief theological sections which preface the very practical body of the report simply assume that the social doctrine of the Trinity is the obvious place to start. Somewhat self-referentially it cites two earlier Church of England reports. Its opening section, 'Theological Principles and Historical Development', quotes directly from the Turnbull Report which claimed, without

17 David Jacobus Bosch, *Transforming Mission: Paradigm Shifts in Theology of Mission* (Maryknoll: Orbis, 1991), e.g. p. 390.

18 This approach is exemplified, for example, by Colin Gunton, *The Promise of Trinitarian Theology* (Edinburgh: T & T Clark, 1993); Colin Gunton, *The One, the Three and the Many: God, Creation and the Culture of Modernity* (Cambridge: Cambridge University Press, 1993); Paul S. Fiddes, *Participating in God: A Pastoral Doctrine of the Trinity* (London: Darton, Longman and Todd, 2000) and Jürgen Moltmann, *The Trinity and the Kingdom of God* (London: SCM Press, 1981).

19 Review Group by the Standing Committee of the General Synod, *Synodical Government in the Church of England: A Review* (London: Church House Publishing, 1997).

20 The report, *Government by Synod* (London: Church Information Office, 1966), deliberately avoided theology since it sought to create a General Synod from the Church Assembly without the need for parliamentary legislation.

explaining precisely how, that the life of the Church was 'utterly Trinitarian in its ground, being and hope'. Thus, the Turnbull Report continued, the Church is 'also firmly part of God's good creation, an assembly of men and women of varying gifts and abilities, who love and support one another through all the joys and difficulties of their daily lives'.[21]

The report on synodical government then goes on to cite the Cameron Report on *Episcopal Ministry* which describes the Church as existing to 'nurture and sustain the relations of human persons joined, as far as it is possible for us as creatures, in a resemblance to that Trinitarian life'.[22] The Church, then, becomes that arena where human beings seek to model the Trinity in all their harmonious relationships. This Trinitarian life – which was also a particular emphasis of the Turnbull Report[23] – was upheld by the gifts of the spirit. The Church is given the capacity to live the divine life as different people embody the diverse gifts given them by the Spirit and use them to build up the common life of the Church. Thus the Turnbull Report suggests at the end of its theological section: 'In a theology of gracious gift the first words must be gratitude, love, service, humility and trust. In such a way the Church can, in its very structures and processes, embody the mission on which it has been sent.'[24] What is conspicuously lacking in the reports, however, is much of a conception of the Church as a political institution riddled with conflict and division and consequently forced to use the dirty ways of the world to make its decisions.

A theological account of synodality, it seems to me, needs to start somewhere else. It cannot begin with the ideal of a mutual relationship of divine love as somehow descriptive of human relationships inside or outside the Church. The reason for that is quite simple:

---

21 Archbishops' Commission on the Organization of the Church of England, *Working as One Body* (London: Church House Publishing, 1995), §1.6.

22 Archbishops' Group on the Episcopate, *Episcopal Ministry* (London: Church House Publishing, 1990), §19.

23 *Working as One Body*, §1.10–25.

24 *Working as One Body*, §1.25.

such language fails to describe the Church as it really is, and is little more than wishful thinking. Instead it seems far better to start by addressing the Church as existing under the conditions of sin. At one point this is even recognized in the Report on Synodical Government. There is an 'acknowledgement of the reality of sin which makes it necessary to have a set of checks and balances in the life of the Church, which will serve to prevent the abuse and power and to preserve the comprehensive nature of the Church'.[25] And yet this reveals an underlying misperception in the Report about the nature and function of the Synod. Rather than making a decision, which may be divisive and express a momentary resolution to an underlying conflict without removing the conflict, a synod is given the task of preserving comprehensiveness. But comprehensiveness may be little more than an Anglican word for conflict. After all, in making a decision it is often the case that one party is simply shown to be wrong, which no amount of pleading for comprehensiveness can conceal. Those who maintained the legitimacy of slavery were not tolerated as what would nowadays be called 'loyal Anglicans'.

Unity, then, is not always a unity in diversity: there will be limits to comprehensiveness. As was brought home in the women bishops' debates of recent years, synods and councils can be cruel things, since making decisions always serves to exclude and alienate those on the losing side, even when they accept the decision, however unwillingly. The somewhat nonsensical language of squaring the circle is predicated on the idea that all truths are as good as all others and that somehow all we have to do is to make a decision that allows people not to accept that a decision was made. This may not always be the best strategy: there are times when mutual indwelling and comprehensiveness are impossible. If that is the case, it might be better to be more realistic and work out a different set of theological principles for the exercise of synodality.

This means that a theology of synodality might be far better rooted in an Augustinian understanding of the Church rather than in the doctrine of the Trinity. For Augustine, as he made clear in his anti-Donatist writings, the Church is a mixed body, a *corpus*

---

25 *Synodical Government in the Church of England*, §2.8.

permixtum,[26] made up of saints and sinners, and because of that it is bound to be a body which is riddled with conflict; there will be competing clamours for authority and assertions of power as the heavenly clashes with the worldly. As an institution both human and divine, the Church needs to work out structures and mechanisms that might better express its identity as the body of Christ, but through all this it remains an institution composed of human beings in all their sinful complexity. So, just because it is a human institution, the body of Christ needs government and constraints: it needs a political theology because it lives under the conditions of human sinfulness. It may be holy but its holiness is always compromised by the issues of power. As the theologian-sociologist David Martin once wrote about Luther:

> Once Luther tried to take monasticism out of the monastery into the world he found the whole enterprise vitiated by a gap, by a break, between the language of the heavenly city and the inherent character of the City of Man. This was hardly a new discovery . . . The malignant worm constantly revisits.[27]

What we know about churches from their long history is that people do not always want to live with one another and sometimes they even want to exclude others from their fellowship. This should come as no surprise: it is something that has been there from the time of St Paul and the Acts of the Apostles. Indeed, I think it would be fair to say that the normal state of the Church is to be in conflict, which is precisely why it needs structures of oversight and some means for institutionalizing conflict and decision-making. The networks of catholicity in the earliest days of the Church emerged not because everybody was in agreement but from precisely the opposite.

---

26 *brev.* 3.20; *c. Don.* 9.12; doc. Chr. 3.32; cf. *civ. Dei* 18.49. The Augustine references are cited according to the schedule in Allan D. Fitzgerald OSA, *Augustine through the Ages: An Encyclopedia* (Grand Rapids MI: Eerdmans, 1999), pp. xxxv–xlix.

27 'The Christian, the Political and the Academic', in David Martin, *On Secularization: Towards a Revised General Theory* (Aldershot: Ashgate, 2005), pp. 185–99, here p. 191.

Legitimacy and Authority

From the very beginning of the Church the question of authority became crucial and was tied up with securing and maintaining the tradition. Increasingly, the authenticity and legitimacy of the tradition were guaranteed by those whose office conferred an authority, but who at the same time were called to their ministry by the local churches and later the local rulers: it was an early truism in the Church that equated the *vox populi* with the *vox dei*. When decisions were made, however, it was usually the case that the divisions continued: all councils and synods could do was to reach agreements at a particular moment of time. The same remains the case: such decisions may or may not be received and may or may not simply lead to further levels of conflict. Synods are unlikely to be structures to build consensus and sometimes their decisions are scarcely important; more frequently they are simply places with rules for engagement which can handle conflict more or less effectively. As Radner writes: 'Councils are not about reaching consensus. Instead, they are about forming a culture of traditions in which actual agreement, in Christian terms, may take place.'[28] Like a parliament, then, a synod will be characterized by a mechanism, or a series of practices, that provides an institutionalization and containment of conflict. Obviously this may not always be the case: sometimes there will be schism and, of course, occasionally there will be consensus and unity. But for the most part the theology of synods will be the study of 'eristology', the theology of divisions and the principles that allow people to live with such divisions without resorting to violence or schism. There is consequently no need to apologize for the fact that the General Synod of the Church of England is political and a place of frequent conflict. This side of the second coming every human institution is bound to be political, the Church no less than the State.

Just as with the politics of the State, so with any ecclesiastical polity the question of legitimacy is central. This is true for all church polities, Presbyterian, congregational or the hybrid

---

28 Radner, *A Brutal Unity*, p. 264.

bishop-in-synod that has eventually been adopted by the Church of England and most other provinces of the Anglican Communion. That means that for synods to work they need to be seen to be legitimate; their authority needs to be accepted by the churches they seek to govern. Any power they wield needs to be connected to those over whom they exercise it. Legitimate authority consequently requires a trust in those political institutions which embody the sorts of mechanisms that might serve to alleviate some of the worst conditions of human sin. With such a degree of trust, synods will become institutions which, while not necessarily removing divisions or resolving conflict, at least help churches learn to live with them.

The Dysfunctionality of Synodical Government in the Church of England

What I think has happened over the past few years, and possibly even longer in the Church of England, however, is that synods have come to be regarded as bodies whose primary task is the promotion of consensus, rather than bodies that allow conflicts to be contained and even used creatively. Synods have become little more than places whose purpose is to support the initiatives of the House of Bishops who have tended to understand their role as a sort of managerial executive standing above the other two houses in promoting unity in the Church. Increasingly they have spoken 'collegially', that is, with one voice, which proved disastrous in the recent debate over the bishops' report on the shared conversations on human sexuality which was discussed in February 2017. This understanding of synods has sometimes resulted in a sense of dysfunctionality. There are some obvious earlier examples which illustrate this approach to synodical government in the Church of England.

First is the rejection of the Anglican Communion Covenant by the majority of English dioceses, which obviously came as an enormous blow to the outgoing Archbishop of Canterbury who had put so much hope in its provisions. Without rehearsing the rights and wrongs of the Covenant, there were particular synodical reasons behind its rejection that had little to do with the matter under discussion: most importantly, the authority of the bishops of the Church of England was at a particularly low ebb in the summer of 2010. To some extent they had brought this upon themselves: their low standing was in part related to the passage of the women bishops' legislation through its earlier stages. The General Synod had appointed a highly qualified and representative group to draft a complex piece of legislation which sought to accommodate as many people as possible without losing the coherence of episcopacy. The Legislative Drafting Group carried with it the authority of the General Synod. However, the two archbishops sought to amend the proposals by making far more concessions to opponents and consequently devaluing the careful legislation that had been prepared: for many, this amounted to an extraordinary breach of trust in the mechanism of the Synod, raising serious questions about the legitimacy of the archbishops' authority as bishops-in-synod. Church leadership was regarded by some as riding roughshod over the judicious institutionalization of conflict which had been impressively demonstrated by the Drafting Group and the Revision Committee. Such a loss of credibility by the House of Bishops – the archbishops were supported by twenty-three other bishops – among significant portions of General Synod made it highly unlikely that the deeply unpopular Covenant proposals would be carried in the dioceses, whatever the bishops thought.

In the subsequent General Synod, in July 2012, the House of Bishops introduced a last-minute amendment to what was intended to be the final debate on the women bishops measure, despite the express instructions from the February Synod not to introduce any substantial amendments. The insertion of this clause served to alienate very many of the supporters of women bishops in General Synod and led to an adjournment of the debate. In the discussion of the Covenant there was very little loyalty shown to many bishops by their own diocesan synods partly because the House of Bishops as a body had failed to respect the legitimate authority of the representative synodical structures in the earlier women bishops' legislation.

Rule by executive diktat with the expectation of consent has not proved a successful episcopal strategy in the past few years. It might be suggested that the Church of England is still living with the consequences: the rare display of near unanimity in the House of Bishops in the unsuccessful November 2012 vote on women bishops was far too late to persuade a highly divided House of Laity into a sense of obedience to the guardians of the faith. Indeed, through the course of the 2010–15 Synod the House of Bishops appeared to be exhibiting what Paul Valliere has recently called 'synodophobia', a word borrowed from the Danish theologian Hans Raun Iversen who developed the term in relation to Denmark's somewhat unusual form of 'churchless Christianity'.[29]

Listening

Alongside such synodophobia has been a parallel series of 'listening' processes that have sought to encourage those who disagree to engage with one another. These have figured prominently in the Church of England and the wider Anglican Communion: the 'listening process' and continuing indaba grew out of successive Lambeth Conferences.[30] More recently a series of shared conversations over two years encouraged by Rowan Williams' leadership of the Church of England and of the Anglican Communion was characterized by a huge effort at listening across the theological divides. As he noted in his retreat addresses given at the Lambeth Conference in 2008, 'the bishop is a linguist' who learns how to speak a language, obeying the rules so that communication occurs. This involves 'listening for the nuances, listening for

---

29 Cited in Paul Valliere, *Conciliarism: A History of Decision-Making in the Church* (Cambridge: Cambridge University Press, 2012), p. 162.

30 The fourteenth conference took place from 16 July to 3 August 2008 with around 670 bishops in attendance. The governing concept for the fourteenth Conference was *indaba*, a word from the African, particularly the Zulu, context. It means a gathering for purposeful discussion in which each voice and the perspectives of all are considered in exploring topics of central importance to the life of the community. The two interwoven themes for the conference were equipping bishops for leadership in mission and strengthening the Communion (from http://www.archbishopofcanterbury.org/pages/lambeth-conference.html).

the hidden music in what someone says or does, listening sometimes for what's beneath the surface as well as what is immediately in front of us. It's a tough experience, and it doesn't happen
quickly.' While ultimately this act of listening requires us first to
listen to the language that emanates from God's Word, it also
requires us to hear the Word in the context of listening to the
other voices around us. This, he claimed, is modelled on Jesus,
who listens to those around him by 'learning our language, listening to our needs, answering our hunger'. Episcopacy was consequently based on the example of Jesus Christ who said something
like this: 'Tell me what your need is, and in giving my love to you
I will be obeying my Father.' The vocation of the bishop was consequently to 'be a Christlike stranger', 'listening for the true need
around us and to hold that together with our listening to God'.
The bishop – and this is presumably equally true for all others
involved in any form of Christian leadership – listens in a 'stereo-
phonic capacity'. He or she 'listens with one ear to the word of
God, and the other to the languages of those among whom he or
she ministers. And somehow the messages come to the one centre
of heart and brain, and we live under the law of Christ.'[31]

This approach to listening might have been all well and good for
the Anglican Communion and the Lambeth Conference, which,
after all, has very few institutionalized mechanisms for listening,
but it seems a high-risk strategy for a church that has developed
complex and carefully constructed mechanisms to ensure that listening happens. In fact, one of the most important characteristics
of General Synod is that it has developed a form of representative
government and a committee structure that, like Parliament, carries a legitimacy that has been conferred on it by the local churches
who trust it to bear their many conflicts. While it might be in need
of reform and the system of elections in the House of Laity may
not be ideal, it nevertheless carries with it a legitimacy which is
conferred by a system of elections and representation. The idea
that a bishop can circumvent Synod and somehow listen 'directly',

---

31 Archbishop's retreat addresses, July 2008 at: http://www
.archbishopofcanterbury.org/articles.php/1739/the-archbishops-retreat-
addresses-parts-iii-iv-v (accessed 2 December 2012).

which resembles the role of the 'special adviser' in the governmental system, can be extremely damaging for the legitimacy of representative government. That, however, seems to be what is possibly implied by the somewhat cryptic statement: 'Tell me what your need is, and in giving my love to you I will be obeying my Father.' Obedience to the Father seems to imply obedience to the 'other' even when that other might be unreasonable, or simply wrong. Something like this, it seems to me, is what happened through the course of the debates over women bishops, and it is perhaps happening in the debates on human sexuality.

Indeed, through almost all his time as archbishop, what Rowan Williams consistently did not do was to force his own views on people – it is as if the task of the bishop forces personal opinions to go 'on hold', and he has to make himself vulnerable to listen to the voice of the other party. Williams has seen his role more as a non-executive chairman of the board than as 'managing director'. His main concern was to listen to those with whom he most disagreed and to find ways of holding them in the traditionally big tent of Anglicanism, even at the risk of losing the confidence of those with whom he agreed. It may be a laudable quality to listen to those of all views and to ensure that there is a sense of openness around the table, but it is usually the loud voices who get to sit at the table in the first place. For a church that has embraced a system of synodical government this seems to be a profoundly risky mechanism: there needs to be trust in that government by all parties, including the bishops. After all, those loud voices, together with many other often quieter voices, are represented – perhaps over-represented – in Synod, and it is through the mechanisms of institutionalized conflict which synods are established to contain that those voices are best heard.

Synodophobia and the Representation of the Laity

The 'synodophobia' of the House of Bishops might indicate a second reason for the rejection of the Anglican Covenant. Because of the vagaries of history and the ways in which the Anglican Communion has developed, the concept of episcopacy that has emerged has frequently failed to give due weight to the role of synods. At a global level episcopal leadership has often been mistaken for episcopal authoritarianism or control. Three of the four instruments of unity have no formal place for laity and the ACC remains a body dominated by bishops and clergy (fifty out of seventy-six members). It is probably for this reason, as Valliere writes, that the view of conciliar or synodical authority 'as inherently antithetical to freedom . . . remains powerful in Anglicanism to this day'.[32] The principle of synodality is scarcely developed in the Anglican Communion structures. This means that for those churches, like the Church of England, that are governed by synods there can be little sense of what might be called 'conciliar legitimacy' for the Instruments of Communion. The laity, who after all pay for the Church, will dislike being told by bishops what they should be doing, whether those bishops are at home or abroad, when they have little or no formal representation. What seems to be required as a necessary precursor to a functioning Covenant is some sort of pan-Anglican synod. As Valliere writes, 'the faltering Anglican Communion needs a worldwide council more than ever'.[33] A council or synod 'would change Anglicanism'[34] by introducing for the first time the principle of lay synodality into the Lambeth Quadrilateral, which, I would suggest, is one of the most misleading documents in Anglican history.[35]

Similarly, within the Church of England, the hard-won rights of the laity cannot be taken for granted. As Archbishop Lang noted in a sermon preached shortly after the creation of the Church Assembly in 1919: 'every man or woman who professes allegiance to the Church is now invested with a personal responsibility for its welfare, for the success or failure of its Divine Mission.' He went on, however, to note that 'all depends upon the spirit, the motive, the purpose, the outlook with which church people enter the new

---

32 Valliere, *Conciliarism*, pp. 192–3.
33 Valliere, *Conciliarism*, p. 209.
34 Valliere, *Conciliarism*, p. 235.
35 See my essay: M. Chapman, 'American Catholicity and the National Church: The Legacy of William Reed Huntington', *Sewanee Theological Review* 56 (2013), 113–48.

era, upon the character which is impressed upon it at its start'.[36] This I think is equally true for the present day in relation to the General Synod as well as the creation of pan-Anglican structures. What seems to be needed is a reinvigoration of an inclusive conciliarism, which bears 'positive witness to the Church as a fellowship transcending office, status and power'.[37] Here I think it is important to note that there are some commentators who have deliberately stressed the continuity of the Church of England through the Reformation, as if somehow the office of bishop stayed much the same: Colin Podmore, the former Clerk of Synod and now chairman of Forward in Faith, for instance, suggested that very little changed in church polity.[38] And yet this understanding needs to be questioned: the submission of the clergy to the Crown, as well as the need for Royal Assent for all new canons, effectively created a lay veto over all church legislation. The Royal Supremacy was rapidly assumed by the Sovereign-in-Parliament, which conferred a second level of legitimacy on the Church of England that derived not from the offices of its episcopal leaders, but from the authority stemming from the episcopally led under a divinely anointed monarch (who appointed the bishops in the first place). With the proroguing of Convocation in 1717 it was Parliament, a predominantly lay body, that gained control of the Church, and obviously through various transitions this authority is now expressed chiefly through the House of Laity in General Synod. Although it would be unwise to make too much of this, it remains true that the authority of General Synod, especially the House of Laity, still derives ultimately from the anointing of a lay woman.[39]

The hard-won freedom of the laity to express its views and opinions was summarized clearly in a letter to Henry Hoare, one of the nineteenth-century pioneers of the lay representation. When synods had spoken, the writer claimed, 'I think that by that time a sufficient substratum of public opinion (in the best sense) will

---

36 Cited in F. A. Iremonger, *William Temple* (London: Oxford University Press, 1948), p. 275.

37 Valliere, *Conciliarism*, p. 112.

38 Colin Podmore, *Aspects of Anglican Identity* (London: Church House Publishing, 2005), p. 103.

39 Kemp, *Counsel and Consent*, pp. 176–231.

have been established, without which no body can act, and against which even Convocation itself . . . would be comparatively powerless.'[40] Moving beyond the British Constitution, it is important to note that the authority and legitimacy of the House of Laity is theologically dependent first and foremost on the notion of the primary vocation of all Christians deriving from their baptismal covenant which is expressed in such an understanding of 'public opinion'. This approach is not without its critics: Colin Podmore, for instance, has been highly critical of the idea of a baptismal covenant as rather too liberal and very American.[41] Such a questioning of baptismal theology has implications for the perception of the legitimacy of the House of Laity in the General Synod in relation to the other houses (even though it is principally the House of Laity that is the heir of parliamentary sovereignty rather than the Upper and Lower Houses of Convocation). It would counter the theological direction of the Synod from its beginning. The 1916 report on Church and State, which led to the setting up of the Church Assembly, for instance, was very clear about the role of the laity: 'It is of great importance to make it plain that when we are pleading for the restoration of autonomy to the Church, we mean the Church and not only the clergy.'[42] It seems to me that the baptismal vocation expressed through representative synods needs to be at the centre of all synods from the PCC to the 'instruments of unity' of the Anglican Communion. This is challenged, however, by the elevation of the 'historic episcopate' above the principle of synodality in the Lambeth Quadrilateral. Historically at least, it is clearly the case that the Church of England's model of authority was based

---

40 Letter from an unnamed correspondent to Hoare, 23 October 1851, in J. B. Sweet, *A Memoir of the late Henry Hoare Esq. MA, with a narrative of the church movements with which he was concerned from 1848 to 1865 and more particularly the revival of Convocation* (London: Rivington's, 1865), p. 308.

41 Colin Podmore, 'The Baptismal Revolution in the American Episcopal Church: Baptismal Ecclesiology and the Baptismal Covenant', *Ecclesiology* 6 (2010), pp. 8–38.

42 The Archbishops' Committee on Church and State, *Report* (London: SPCK, 1916), p. 31. It drew extensively on the earlier 1902 report on the laity in the Church.

on the predominantly lay veto of Parliament and later the General Synod rather than the authority of the historic episcopate.[43] A theological justification rests in a shared baptism and seems urgently required for the future of the Anglican Communion as it develops into a synodical and representative church from a loose federation united – or disunited – around the 'historic episcopate'.

Conclusion

What emerges from this discussion is a theology of General Synod that locates it in a political theology of institutionalized conflict which finds its origins in Augustine of Hippo's understanding of the Church. General Synod, like other synods, is a political body established to bear the divisions and conflicts that are an inherent part of the human condition, and is not some imaginary sub-Trinitarian love-fest which aims at consensus-building or expressing Anglican comprehensiveness, whatever that means.[44] If we have a theologically grounded mechanism of institutionalized conflict, which is representative of the Church, it is to that body alone that we should entrust our decision-making. The bishops – like the government – have an honoured place in the process, but their respect and their trust have to be won through co-operation and engagement with the representative body. Autocracy, however divinely established, is not a good way of gaining friends and influencing people, especially when they are the ones who are paying their dues. Synods may not be ideal but that is how the Church of England has chosen to manage its conflicts this side of eternity. The bishops have a constitutional role and a power of veto, but they have to learn the art of trust and the politics of compromise, and they also need to learn the art of public disagreement rather than an imposed collegiality that few in the other two houses will ever believe to be much more than an effort to avoid conflict at any cost.

---

43 Mark Chapman, *Bishops, Saints and Politics: Anglican Essays* (London: T & T Clark, 2007), pp. 9–32.

44 See Mark Chapman, *Anglican Theology* (London: Continuum, 2012), ch. 1.

3

Historical Research and Modern Anglican Worship[1]

PAUL F. BRADSHAW

One of my fellow liturgical scholars, whose identity I had better not reveal, is convinced that I have an ulterior motive behind all my research into the liturgical practices of early Christians, and that is to bring about the elimination from present-day worship of everything that did not exist in the first few centuries, in other words to exercise a kind of liturgical fundamentalism and restore some sort of primitive purity to our modern practice. Quite apart from the practical impossibility of such an undertaking, nothing could be further from my mind. We don't accuse those doing secular archaeological research of wanting to make us all live in the ancient houses that they uncover, so why does an interest in our distant liturgical past immediately raise the suspicion that those of us on liturgical commissions and the like are bent on undoing centuries of tradition?

Indeed, as we shall see, although appearances might suggest that liturgical revisers in the twentieth century were trying to restore primitive liturgical practices to Anglican worship, in fact their real motivations often lay elsewhere. I have demonstrated in a recent article published in *Theology* that the introduction of the offertory procession to the standard practices of the Parish Communion movement did not stem from a desire to imitate what was thought to be the universal practice in early Christianity but from a desire to give expression to the theological conviction that the Eucharist was the offering by the people of themselves. It was only in the

---

1 A lecture given at the Community of the Resurrection, Mirfield, May 2017, as part of the celebration of the 125th anniversary of its foundation.

thinking of Gregory Dix and others like him that its resemblance to seventh-century papal practice was adduced and the claim made that this therefore had been the custom of the Church everywhere in the first few centuries, in spite of a complete lack of evidence for this, and in the face of at least one piece of evidence to the contrary.[2] The existence of such a pedigree mattered to them, but not to everyone else. Whether a procession by a few chosen people moving bread and wine from one place in the church to another really does effectively symbolize the people's offering, except to certain clergy, is of course another matter altogether.

Something similar was also true of the introduction of the parish breakfast after the service in some early Parish Communion parishes. Its purpose was not to reproduce the early Christian agape meal but to try to preserve the tradition of fasting before communion, as it was feared that those attending this somewhat later celebration of Holy Communion than was usual might otherwise be tempted to have breakfast first – yes, many clergy worried about that sort of thing in the first half of the twentieth century. It was certainly recognized at the same time that it did offer the additional benefit of an opportunity for fellowship between members of the congregation, which is presumably why a remnant of it has survived down to the present day, usually in the form of watery instant coffee in the church hall after the service. However, because in most places only a limited number of the congregation usually choose to stay on for this activity, once again it is questionable whether it can really be said to provide the element of fellowship and interpersonal relationships otherwise absent from our parish Eucharist.

The Exchange of the Peace

Even what is usually called the exchange of the Peace did not originate directly from imitation of what was thought to have been

---

2 Paul F. Bradshaw, 'Gregory Dix and the Offertory Procession', *Theology* 120 (2017), pp. 27–33.

early Christian practice. It was not part of the earlier phase of the Parish Communion movement but was eventually introduced into Anglican worship via the liturgy of the Church of South India, first authorized in 1954. The immediate motivation for its inclusion in the South Indian service was the desire to incorporate elements from all the churches that were participating in the new united Church, and this particular ceremony was part of the rite of the St Thomas Christians in India, descendants from the ancient Syrian Church. So it does have its ultimate roots in early Christian practice, but its modern adoption did not come directly from there.

While the South India rite had prescribed a specific hand gesture based on the normal South Indian social greeting, and also directed that it was to be passed formally from the presiding minister through those assisting to other members of the congregation, when it appeared for the first time in an authorized English liturgy, Series 3 in 1973, the direction that they might be accompanied 'with a handclasp or similar action' and both 'passed through the congregation' was added. However, when the Alternative Service Book appeared in 1980 the option of exchanging what was called 'a sign of peace' still included, it was without any indication as to what form that might take. In practice, both in England and throughout the Anglican Communion, the gesture usually became a handshake, and the exchange was generally made informally between those sitting near to one another or, in some cases, by everyone moving about the worship space to exchange it with every other person present, and not in the more formal South Indian way.

Thus, the physical gesture was not only different from that employed in South India but also different from that used by early Christians. For, as scholars were well aware, the early Christians had actually exchanged a kiss with one another, apparently on the lips. When I explain this to Anglican congregations, I swear I can see them shrinking back in their pews, thinking, 'He's going to make us do it!' More than this difference in form, however, is the difference in meaning that was attached to it. In modern practice, it is all about peace. In the South Indian rite it was simply labelled 'the Peace', and that term has stuck with it everywhere else that the ceremony has been adopted. But that was not so in early Christianity. It was always 'the kiss' and although the word 'peace' was sometimes associated with it, it was not invariably so: in the New Testament, for example, it was known as the 'holy kiss'.[3] And the point was that in Graeco-Roman culture, kisses were usually exchanged only between members of one's immediate family or very close friends, not indiscriminately with everyone that one met. So, for Christians to indulge in so intimate a gesture with one another was both shocking to outsiders and a sign that they regarded other Christians as their true brothers and sisters. Indeed, some even refused any longer to kiss those members of their biological family who were not baptized. It was thus a highly symbolic and counter-cultural act. In our own culture, however, shaking hands doesn't carry anything like that meaning. It is important to note, therefore, that in this case, as in the case of the offertory procession, modern revisers have changed not only the outward form but also the interpretation of the historical precedent. So it is not true to say, as many have done, that we are 'doing what the early Church did'. We are performing a significantly different action with a quite different meaning. This doesn't of course mean that it is wrong: just different.

The Eucharistic Prayer

This brings us to a significant point about the use of historical research in modern Anglican worship. We generally do not simply copy the past, but we adapt and reinterpret it in our different cultural and theological situation. Another good example of this is the way that many modern eucharistic rites have tried to incorporate the eucharistic prayer found in the so-called *Apostolic Tradition* of Hippolytus. There was such a rush to do this forty to fifty years ago because it was thought to have been *the* eucharistic prayer of the Church in Rome in the early third century. What better pedigree could a prayer have than that, for those

3 Rom. 16.16; 1 Cor. 16.20; 2 Cor. 13.12; 1 Thess. 5.26. See further L. Edward Phillips, *The Ritual Kiss in Early Christian Worship*, Alcuin/GROW Joint Liturgical Study 36 (Cambridge: Grove Books, 1996); Michael Philip Penn, *Kissing Christians: Ritual and Community in the Late Ancient Church* (Philadelphia: University of Pennsylvania Press, 2005).

who needed that sort of justification? Unfortunately, more recent scholarship, including my own writing, has cast serious doubts on the authorship, date and character of that ancient anonymous document, and in particular suggested that the eucharistic prayer in it was a secondary addition to the text, very likely not added to it until sometime in the early fourth century from somewhere in west Syria. This would still make it quite old, but certainly not the ancient prayer of the Roman Church.[4]

Regardless of that scholarly debate, however, we should note what all modern revisers, and not just those in the Anglican Communion, did with it. They did not reproduce it word for word, but modified it to make it resemble more strongly the traditions of eucharistic praying that they were already familiar with. In particular, with – I think – the sole exception of the Evangelical Lutheran Church in America, everyone added a Sanctus to the prayer; the Roman Catholic Church and most Anglican provinces inserted an invocation of the Holy Spirit on the bread and wine *before* the narrative of institution, in order to give expression to the traditional Western theory that it was the words of Jesus at the Last Supper that effected the consecration; and most churches other than the Roman Catholic tried to find some way of avoiding using the words 'we offer', even though they occurred in the original. Indeed, the Roman Catholic Church made so many changes and additions that at least one Roman Catholic scholar has commented that his Church's version is virtually a completely new prayer.[5]

What Christians Have Always Done

Are such blatant alterations and adaptations of former practices legitimate? Should we not seek to be true to ancient traditions?

---

4 See, for example, Paul F. Bradshaw, Maxwell E. Johnson and L. Edward Phillips, *The Apostolic Tradition: A Commentary*, Hermeneia Commentary Series (Minneapolis: Fortress Press, 2002).

5 Matthieu Smyth, 'The Anaphora of the So-Called Apostolic Tradition and the Roman Eucharistic Prayer', in *Issues in Eucharistic Praying*, ed. Maxwell E. Johnson (Collegeville: Liturgical Press, 2011) pp. 71–97.

The first important point we need to remember is that what we have been doing in the last hundred years is in fact exactly what Christians have always done. Liturgical practices have always changed and adapted to changed situations, at some times quite slowly and at other times more rapidly, but the notion of an unchanging liturgy until modern revisers got their hands on it is a complete myth. Let me illustrate this with just a couple of examples.

First, the *pedilavium* or foot-washing ceremony. This first emerges to our sight in the late fourth century, when it formed part of the baptismal rite in northern Italian dioceses. In this context it was obviously focused on those being baptized also having their feet washed and not on the one performing the action, as they sought to fulfil Christ's saying to Peter in John's Gospel that, 'If I do not wash your feet, you have no part in me' (John 13.4–10). Later it became associated instead with Maundy Thursday, not as part of the liturgy but chiefly in monastic houses and cathedral chapters, where the head of the community washed the feet of the rest. Not only had the context changed, but so had the meaning, as it now focused on the one performing the action, showing how the great could display the humility of Jesus by stooping to wash the feet of lesser mortals. The British monarchy later still inserted a further twist when, in the eighteenth century, they stopped bending the knee and started instead to hand out money, a symbol of their largesse rather than of their humility.

It was not until the 1950s that it finally became part of the Holy Thursday liturgy in the Roman Catholic Church, where its meaning changed yet again to something new: what the late Bishop Kenneth Stevenson called a piece of 'representational liturgy',[6] an acting out of a biblical scene, like those churches that bring a real donkey into church on Palm Sunday. Twelve embarrassed-looking lay people, who have volunteered – or more often been reluctantly persuaded to come forward – have their feet washed by the clergy. From there it has spread into many Anglican churches in this form, although more progressive parishes in the Episcopal

---

6 Kenneth Stevenson, *Jerusalem Revisited: The Liturgical Meaning of Holy Week* (Washington DC: Pastoral Press, 1988), pp. 9–10.

Church in the USA have gone further and given it yet another new form and new meaning. Instead of being something that the rest of the congregation simply watch, they have invited everyone to participate, first having their own feet washed before washing the feet of the person next in line, thus giving a quasi-sacramental expression to the Christian truth that only when we are willing to receive are we in a position to give to others. Hence, different forms and different meanings throughout history.

My second example is the rite of confirmation. In spite of having the appearance of a post-baptismal laying-on of hands associated with the Holy Spirit in the book of Acts, it is only in North Africa and at Rome in the third century that something similar occurs and not in other parts of the ancient Christian world. By the end of the fourth century at Rome the imposition of hands had been changed into an anointing with oil and began to be separable from baptism. In the following centuries the Roman practice was adopted throughout the Western Church and the separation became a matter of years, and so a new meaning was needed to explain it. It was now understood not as the initial baptism in the Spirit but a further gift of the Spirit in order to strengthen the Christian on his or her journey through life – a booster shot, if you like. In the sixteenth century the Reformers restored the imposition of hands and came up with yet another meaning for the ceremony – which they of course believed was its original biblical meaning – that it was the occasion for the candidates to confirm their faith. Modern Roman Catholic practice has been to combine these latter two interpretations, as has much Anglican practice.

Once again, different forms and different meanings throughout history. As I indicated before, the notion of an unchanging liturgy until modern revisers got their hands on it is a complete myth. At one time it was popular to look to the liturgy of the Orthodox Church as embodying such changelessness, but while it is true that Orthodox worship has preserved some elements from ancient times that Western rites lost, Eastern liturgies underwent development and change for many centuries just as much as Western ones did. Similarly, claims that what is now called the Extraordinary Form of the Roman Rite has been unchanged for over a thousand years are equally wide of the mark. It is certainly true that the core prayers in that rite have remained constant, but that is certainly not the case with regard to many of the subsidiary elements and above all of the manner and style of its celebration, which has gone through all sorts of variations. Even the eucharistic rite in the Book of Common Prayer came to be celebrated in quite different ways in the course of its history and in many cases without word-for-word adherence to the written text, as any priest who has ever turned up in a different parish to take what the locals say is just the Prayer Book service will be able to tell you.

Misunderstanding History

All of this changing and adaptation of traditional practices through the centuries certainly does not mean that the attempt was never made to return to earlier custom. Hence the second important point we need to remember is this: often the intention of the changes was precisely to do that. As a Jewish colleague of mine once remarked, those attempting a radical alteration to the tradition frequently have to convince others that what they are proposing is even more traditional than that which the traditionalists are defending. Thus, the sixteenth-century Reformers were sure that what they were initiating was a return to the patterns of worship of the New Testament; and the Roman Catholic reformers at the Council of Trent were attempting to strip away many of the accretions that had attached themselves to the various medieval rites in order to return to a purer Roman tradition. In both cases, however, their success was limited by the extent of historical scholarship at the time. Similarly, although the twentieth-century reformers of Anglican liturgies may not have had as their primary objective recreating the liturgy of the early Church exactly as it had been, they certainly drew on and were influenced in the decisions that they made by what they knew of early Christian worship practices, even though they too were constrained both by the limitations of academic research at the time and also by seeing in ancient Christianity the things they wanted to see and not seeing those that they didn't want to find there.

For example, they understood the holy kiss in ancient Christianity as primarily conveying reconciliation and peace – it was after all the 1960s – and so took that aspect from it while discarding – or being unaware of – the rest. Similarly, on the basis of the scholarship of the time, they thought that the eucharistic prayer in the supposed *Apostolic Tradition* of Hippolytus had been *the* eucharistic prayer of the Roman Church in the third century, and probably earlier still, and so gave it a position of historical pre-eminence that it really doesn't deserve. A further example of such limitation of historical knowledge was the notion that Easter was the normative occasion for baptism in early Christianity. This view was also encouraged by the common assumption in twentieth-century liturgical scholarship that whatever had been the practice in the city of Rome must have been the norm for the whole of Christianity, with any variant customs elsewhere being deviations that were not to be trusted or imitated. So, on the basis of the early Roman tradition, we have all been pressed to think that Easter is the ideal occasion for holding baptisms, and indeed in theory should be the only time in the year for baptisms, if only we could persuade difficult parents to consent to it. More recent research, however, has shown us that only at Rome and in North Africa was there a preference for Easter baptism – and note that it was *only* a preference – before the fourth century, and not anywhere else in early Christianity, and that even when an attempt was made in the fourth century to make it normative everywhere, that did not hold, and in less than fifty years had effectively been abandoned in practice, even if it lived on in theory.[7] That is a very weak historical foundation on which to build modern practice. This is not to say, however, that there may not be other good reasons to encourage baptisms at Easter, but I will return to that later.

---

7 See Paul F. Bradshaw, '"Diem baptismo sollemniorem": Initiation and Easter in Christian Antiquity', in *Eulogêma: Studies in Honor of Robert Taft, S.J.*, ed. Ephrem Carr, Stefano Parenti, Abraham-Andreas Thiermeyer and Elena Velkovska, Studia Anselmiana 110 (Rome: Pontificio Ateneo S. Anselmo, 1993), pp. 41–51; reprinted in Maxwell E. Johnson (ed.), *Living Water, Sealing Spirit: Readings on Christian Initiation* (Collegeville: Liturgical Press, 1995), pp. 137–47.

Reading by Lay People

As a final example of misunderstanding history, let us take a look at the alleged right of lay people to read the lessons in church. Now, there was an ancient tradition in the Church of England of the Parish Clerk reading the Epistle in the Eucharist,[8] and in 1866 the office of lay reader was formally recognized, so that in one sense it can be said that the practice of lay people participating in the readings had already been well established in Anglicanism prior to the modern liturgical movement. But these earlier instances were all of appointed lay officers, not lay people in general. At some point in the second half of the twentieth century, however, it began to be asserted that reading belonged to lay people by right, simply by being lay people, regardless of an official appointment or even the presence of proven ability to read well in public. But this once more flew in the face of historical precedent. Reading in church in early Christianity had always been done by those appointed to particular ministries, so while it is true to say that reading was certainly not the exclusive prerogative of the priest, that does not mean that it was therefore thought of as a right belonging to all lay people. That would be rather like saying that because playing the organ is not something the priest alone can do, therefore every lay person should be free to have a go. On the contrary, making music and public reading are things belonging to those able to do them.

Continuity with the Past

Thus, we have established that change and adaptation have been characteristic of Christian worship throughout its history, and that although such changes have often involved attempts to

---

8 See for example Cuthbert F. Atchley, *The Parish Clerk and his Right to Read the Liturgical Epistle*, Alcuin Club Tracts 4 (London: Longmans, Green and Co., 1903).

recapture elements from its earlier times that had been lost, they were often affected by lack of accurate historical knowledge or by misunderstanding of the data. Does this situation then suggest that historical research has no effective contribution to make to modern Anglican worship, that we can largely ignore history when producing forms for our own day? I want to suggest reasons why this should not be so.

First, some continuity with our past is a necessity for Christianity. Our faith is rooted, not in specific doctrines, but in our historical origins. Tradition may turn and twist as it wends its way through history, but it is what connects us to our foundations, and our worship needs also to anchor us in that. Liturgical revision therefore might be compared to the redevelopment of a city centre. Provided that some of the original architectural features are retained, people can still feel at home and find their way about; but if the whole area is cleared and rebuilt, there is nothing left to act as markers to the familiar.

A response to this might be: 'Well, then, provided we keep the essentials of Christian worship described in the New Testament, surely we can then be free to do as we wish about the rest?' I regret, however, that it is not as easy to accomplish that as it sounds, partly because of the enormous differences in culture between then and now, and partly because our knowledge of the practice of those days is still only partial, with large gaps remaining in it. So my fellow scholar who fears that this is my real aim need have no worries on that score. But there is even more to it than that, because it is not a simple matter to distinguish core elements of New Testament worship that should be preserved from the more peripheral that we can readily ignore. This sort of attempt always involves considerable subjective judgement about what is essential and what is not, and usually ends up with people creating the past in their own image rather than in fidelity to the actual historical evidence. Cyprian of Carthage in the mid-third century appears to be the very first to argue that the priest should do exactly what Jesus did at the Last Supper, but even he was forced to admit that Jesus did it in the evening while Cyprian's church celebrated the Eucharist in the morning, and unwilling – or unable – to change that, he had to try to come up with a rationale to justify the difference: he said that it is because *we* are celebrating the resurrection.[9]

The same sort of fate awaits any others to try to balance what they read in the New Testament and other early Christian evidence with what their own theology or cultural traditions tell them is right for the Eucharist. I recently reviewed a book that was seeking to restore the essentials of the earliest Eucharist in the present day. The author believed it should be in the context of an evening meal shared in houses by small groups, eaten sitting down and not standing, and involving ordinary bread and ordinary wine, with the latter in individual cups, all this because it is what he thought Jesus intended and the earliest believers practised, from which ideal later Christian history had marked a drastic decline. But he did not think that we needed to do everything that they did. He knew that early Christians exchanged a kiss in their gatherings, but thought it sufficient if we just express fellowship in some way. He knew that the unbaptized were excluded from communion, but he wanted to change that rule to extend to baptized Christians who are not true believers. He knew that standing to receive communion was an early practice, but thought we did not have to replicate that either. He admitted that a common cup was in use among some second-century congregations, but regarded this as connected with the mistaken belief in a change taking place in the elements, and above all as much too unhygienic to be employed today.

Later Developments Not Necessarily Wrong

In any case, it would be a mistake to treat *all* later developments in liturgical practice as illegitimate, as somehow a departure from the purity of apostolic worship, in other words to engage in what I called earlier a sort of liturgical fundamentalism. For example, as far as we know, early Christian Eucharists did not include any expression of penitence within them. Indeed, the widespread

---

9 Cyprian, *Letter* 63.16.

prohibition against kneeling on a Sunday would have prevented any act of penitence at all on that day. Modern liturgical enthusiasts have unconsciously and mistakenly converted that into a rule about merely standing for the eucharistic prayer – which of course was not its original meaning at all. Nevertheless, who would now want to eliminate all penitential rites from Sunday worship just because they were not part of early Christian practice? Or take, for a second example, the renewal of baptismal vows, either at the Easter Vigil or on some other occasion. This has no place in earlier Christian tradition but is entirely a mid-twentieth-century invention, part of the Roman Catholic revision of Holy Week rites in the 1950s. Again, who would now want to eliminate it on the grounds that it was not part of traditional practice?

It is not relative age alone, therefore, that ought to determine whether or not something should have a place in present-day worship, but its theological value. When we attempt to recover things from the past, we should not be engaging in mere antiquarianism but doing so because they embody things that we believe and give better expression to them than our current practice does. Let us go back to baptism at Easter that I referred to earlier. We cannot go on saying that we are promoting it simply because 'that's what the early Church did', because we now know that only some early Christians practised it and that it did not really take on for very long anywhere because of the high infant mortality rate. But we can promote it because we believe its theological message that being baptized is participating sacramentally in dying and rising with Christ. In other words, there are good doctrinal reasons for the practice and not just historical evidence. That does not mean that it is the only correct occasion for baptism and that therefore we can criticize others who do not follow the custom for not doing it right. As Tertullian, our earliest witness to the practice, himself said, every day is suitable for baptism.[10] And there are other, equally valid, New Testament theologies of baptism than the Romans 6 motif of dying and rising with Christ, and so we have no justification to grant preferential status to that alone.

---

10 Tertullian, *De baptismo* 19.

To take another example that we touched on earlier, the *pedilavium* or foot-washing. We may believe that its most valuable purpose for our congregation is to help to visualize something that happened long ago and far away. But think for a moment of the nativity play at Christmas. We don't usually hire a troupe of actors to come and perform it for our congregation so that we can visualize better the circumstances of the birth of Christ. Instead we get the children to act it out. The aim of that, of course we have to admit, is partly to attract their parents to come to church to watch it, but the real reason is so that the children can experience it by participating and not just spectating, because entering into it is much more profound for them than just watching others. In the same way, sacramental participation in foot-washing by the whole congregation is a much more profound experience than simply seeing others do it. That is why even getting people reluctantly to shake hands with one another in a church service has a greater impact than letting them stand there without touching, even if the impact turns out to be simply their realization that they do not really want to be a member of the body of Christ and to relate to other people after all, but prefer to keep their religion private and individual!

Good historical research, therefore, serves to warn us against false interpretations of the past, against reading our own preferences and predilections into the traditions we have inherited, or misusing the claim that 'we are doing what the early Church did' in order to justify something we want to introduce. But at the same time, it should not prevent us from adapting and developing those traditions in new ways to give expression to what we now believe, provided that we do not confuse the two.

But good historical research is not there simply to prevent us from making errors of interpretation or false attribution. Historical research can also open our eyes to practices of the past of which we had hitherto been unaware, and so offer us alternative visions for our liturgical future. It can teach us that things have not always been the way they are now, but that there was once a time when Christians did things differently, and understood their worship practices differently. We are not obliged to copy them, but we can learn from them. The ultimate criterion for our worship is not history, but theology illuminated by history. Therefore, I end with this quotation from Robert Taft, probably the greatest liturgical scholar alive today: 'The past is always instructive, but not necessarily normative. What we do today is not ruled by the past but by the adaptation of the tradition to the needs of the present. History can only help us decide what the essentials of that tradition are, and the parameters of its adaptation.'[11]

---

11 Robert F. Taft, *The Liturgy of the Hours in East and West* (Collegeville: Liturgical Press, 1986), pp. xiv–xv.

4

A Liturgical Revolution

STEPHEN PLATTEN

What Revolution?

There are moments in people's lives when new perceptions form or their world is viewed from a dramatically different perspective. The distinguished philosopher of religion, and later Bishop of Durham, Dr Ian Ramsey, talked of moments when the 'penny drops' or the 'ice breaks'.[1] Somehow one's world, at least some aspect of it, is refashioned. Just one such moment remains vividly in my mind in relation to how I understood the power and significance of the liturgy. As members of staff at the former theological college in Lincoln, in the 1980s, we all welcomed a new lecturer in liturgy, one Robert Gribben. It was a twofold welcome since he would also be filling the slot of Lincoln's Methodist Ecumenical Lectureship. Gribben, nurtured as a Methodist, was now de facto a minister in the Uniting Church in Australia. He brought to his new role at Lincoln a panache and creativity admired by all. So, for example, almost everyone was helped to see the liturgical journey from Candlemas to Easter in an utterly new light.[2] The dramatic contrasts in the use of colour for the seasons, the use of light and darkness and an imaginative choreography of the liturgy radically affected people's perception. It was a fascinating irony that catholic-minded Anglicans had their perceptions of the liturgy refocused by someone who ostensibly came from a church

---

1 See, for example, Ian Ramsey, *Models for Divine Activity* (London: SCM Press, 1973); Ian Ramsey, *Models and Mystery* (London: Oxford University Press, 1964).

2 See R. W. Gribben, *Rite on Time*: *Recovering the Roots of Christian Worship Today* (Melbourne: Forum, 1993).

born from a historical divorce from the Church of England in the eighteenth century: the Methodist Church.

The impact of these new perceptions was sharply focused in one season after another, in different festivals and even sometimes in the manner in which the daily office and Eucharist were celebrated. It was during this time at Lincoln that the Paschal Vigil and Eucharist were first reintroduced in their fullness, with the dramatic contrasts using different genres of music interspersed between the solemn readings recounting creation and redemption. The college, in successive years, celebrated the Vigil after dark on Holy Saturday and then next time at dawn on Easter Morning. An Ulster Anglican, who had never experienced such a celebration before, reflected that it was the most *missionary* service he had ever attended.

Gribben's impact must, of course, be partly put down to both his scholarship and to his extraordinary talent as a teacher. The phenomenon described, however, was also effectively part of a far wider shift whose roots are traceable back even to the nineteenth century. It was chiefly in the twentieth century, however, that this shift, this burgeoning liturgical movement, flowered. It has effectively ushered in a liturgical revolution. Such a revolution is not unique to liturgical nor indeed even to theological development. In 1962, Thomas Kuhn, the American physicist, historian and philosopher of science, wrote a ground-breaking book[3] about the nature of scientific development. He argued that, over the centuries, science has continued within one paradigm and without significant change; he called this *normal science*. Every so often, however, there will be a series of breakthroughs that, coming together, result in a paradigm shift; this heralds *revolutionary science*. Examples would include the Copernican revolution in astronomy, Newton's work on gravity and the laws of motion, Darwin and Wallace on evolution and Einstein on relativity. Many of the old patterns either break down or morph, producing a new paradigm. Of course, what went before was crucial, hence Newton's famous *bon mot* in relation to his significant discoveries

---

3 Thomas S. Kuhn, *The Structure of Scientific Revolutions* (Chicago: University of Chicago Press, 1962).

that, 'If I have seen further, it is by standing on the shoulders of giants.'

Liturgical development can, to some degree, be seen in a similar light. Effectively the first revolution was the earliest *evolution* of the liturgy, as we now understand it, in sub-apostolic times. Elements of liturgical worship appear to be caught in the aspic of the New Testament, but it was in the *Didache* and other texts within sub-apostolic literature that this development emerged and contributed to Patristic patterns. Another obvious time of liturgical revolution was at the Reformation; and then later, of course, the modern liturgical movement, to which we have already alluded. These have been broad-sweeping periods of revolution, but other limited examples would include the Iconoclastic controversy in the East, with the subsequent restoration of icons at the second Council of Nicaea in 787; the eventual emergence in the eighteenth and nineteenth centuries of Methodist liturgical worship, including the Covenant Service; and also, ironically, the evolution of patterns of worship among the Society of Friends.[4]

The Liturgical Movement

What in summary, then, should be noted of the 'modern liturgical movement'? The work of Guéranger in nineteenth-century France was seminal, even though Guéranger was himself opposed to liturgical diversity; A. G. Martimort, Louis Bouyer and Joseph Gelineau followed in the twentieth century. It was, perhaps in Germany that the most crucial work emerged. The Beuronese Congregation of Benedictines (Beuron is north of Lake Constance in Baden-Württemberg), founded in the mid-nineteenth century, under the influence of Solesmes Abbey in France and Maredsous in Belgium, were pioneers. This same congregation refounded the Benedictine Abbey at Maria Laach in the Rheinland just before

---

4 Interesting insights into this counter-intuitive notion of Quaker liturgy are collected together in Pink Dandelion, *The Liturgies of Quakerism* (Aldershot: Ashgate, 2005).

the turn of the twentieth century. Here the key figures were Dom Odo Casel, and the diocesan priest, Romano Guardini. Casel was the crucial figure in underpinning the theological foundations with his so-called 'mystery theology';[5] he sought to re-establish a rich understanding of the Eucharist and the manner in which the Eucharist both 'makes' and 'manifests' the Church, and is indeed also the foundation of the individual's living and praying of the gospel. Again, in a most subtle manner, the liturgy is ineluctably *missionary* in its performance.

So, here were the seeds for a new flowering in liturgical theology, but here too began innovative and constructive practice. These two elements together provoked a new attitude to both the structuring and performance of the liturgy. In Kuhn's terms, here was a clear paradigm shift, a revolution. It was a shift that would be manifested and flower most richly in the middle years of the twentieth century, and notably with the Second Vatican Council.

Vatican II and Liturgical Renewal

It is almost impossible to exaggerate the overall impact of the Second Vatican Council not only on the Roman Catholic Church, but also in its 'knock-on' effects within other Christian communions.[6] The key Council documents relating to worship and liturgy were the *Dogmatic Constitution on the Church in the Modern World*,[7] the *Decree on Ecumenism*,[8] the *Dogmatic Constitution on the Nature of the Church*[9] and the *Constitution*

---

5 Odo Casel, *The Mystery of Christian Worship*, trans. and ed. Burkhand Neunhauser OSB (London: Darton, Longman and Todd, 1962). Casel's work is notoriously opaque and the translation here does not help. An interpretation of Casel's theology lies at the heart of George Guiver, *Pursuing the Mystery* (Mirfied: Mirfield Publications, 2016).

6 See here Stephen Platten, 'Selling a Tiara, Giving a Ring: Paul VI's Jewelled Legacy', *Theology* 119:6 (2016), pp. 407–16.

7 *Vatican II: The Conciliar and Post-Conciliar Documents*, revised edition (New York: Costello, 1988), I, pp. 903ff.

8 *Vatican II: The Conciliar and Post-Conciliar Documents*, pp. 452ff.

9 *Vatican II: The Conciliar and Post-Conciliar Documents*, pp. 350ff.

on the Sacred Liturgy:[10] all have been foundational. In an insti-
tutional/ecclesiastical sense they are further manifestations of
the paradigm shift already noted. The translation of the liturgy
into the vernacular was but the beginning. The recovery of the
Eucharist as a *celebration* of the entire eucharistic community
over which the priest *presides* led to the wholesale reordering of
churches across the world. The revised liturgies for Holy Week
and the Triduum sparked off completely new understandings of
the nature of Christian worship, not only among Roman Catholics
but far more broadly.

Even within the Roman Catholic Church itself, these revisions
and changes have not been uncontroversial. Piero Marini, who
was the head of the Office for the Liturgical Celebrations of the
Supreme Pontiff from 1987 to 2007, has set out the background
to this as he saw it. As personal secretary to Archbishop Annibale
Bugnini he was closely involved in the work of the Concilium
that was charged with the task of implementing liturgical reform.
He later became secretary of the reconfigured Congregation for
Divine Worship. Marini has documented this entire process in his
book describing the development of reform.[11] He notes towards
the end of his book that the Congregation for Divine Worship
changed its name once again in 1975 to the Congregation for
Divine Worship and the Discipline of the Sacraments:

'This was probably one of the first signs of a tendency to return
to a preconciliar mindset that has for years now characterised the
Curia's approach. As more and more time passes since the Second
Vatican Council, an event charged with such hope and renewal,
its distinctive contribution seems to be increasingly questioned.'[12]

John Baldovin in his useful response to this critical backlash
reviews a number of different commentators who have questioned
the reforms. He concludes:

---

10 *Vatican II: The Conciliar and Post-Conciliar Documents*, pp. 1ff.
11 Piero Marini, *A Challenging Reform: Realizing the Vision of the
Liturgical Renewal* (Collegeville: Liturgical Press, 2007).
12 Marini, *A Challenging Reform*, p. 157.

with regard to the Church's worship there is no going back. Antiquarianism can take many forms and today it seems often to assume that of nostalgia for a beautiful mediaeval dream of a liturgy, a liturgy that took place in the Ages of Faith. That world – and therefore that liturgy – are gone. It will do no good to try to retrieve them.[13]

The pontificate of Francis I has thus far augured well for a recovery of the Vatican II conciliar spirit. Nonetheless, despite these criticisms and critiques, the centralized patterns of authority within the Church have meant that such changes have been universally received.[14] The recent over-literal revised version of the liturgy is a relatively small shift in contrast to the Vatican II reforms.

Interestingly enough, the Church of England's Liturgical Commission, established by the Church Assembly to review liturgical provision, preceded Vatican II by some eight years. It was set up in 1955 to look to the renewal of worship. Again, the work of the Commission would build upon earlier insights, and notably Anglican scholarship from earlier in the century. Henry de Candole and Gabriel Hebert both introduced some of the work of the mainland continental pioneers, notably Odo Casel and Lambert Beauduin (from the Belgian monastery now known as Chèvetogne).

Hebert had been influenced by the work of F. D. Maurice. In his book *Liturgy and Society* Hebert laid out the foundations of his thought, drawing widely on the work of mainland continental theologians. Worship was, he was clear, central to Christian life since the Christian religion is not simply an individualized and private religion. Hebert was concerned to recover the corporate nature of worship; it is the liturgy which identifies the nature of the Church. This recovery of the corporate nature of worship, together with the realization that worship was one of the foundations of the Parish and People Movement, encouraged the development of

---

13 John F. Baldovin, *Reforming the Liturgy: A Response to the Critics* (Collegeville: Liturgical Press, 2008), p. 157.

14 For an excellent survey, see Marini, *A Challenging Reform*. Archbishop Marini was head of the Office for Liturgical Celebrations of the Supreme Pontiff (1987–2007). See also Baldovin, *Reforming the Liturgy* for a balanced review of critics of the reforms.

what later became known as the Parish Communion Movement. Indeed, Hebert's other key book at this point was titled simply *The Parish Communion*. Christopher Irvine comments:

> Further theoretical and practical consideration regarding the programme for the renewal of worship were offered in the essays contained in Hebert's symposiums *The Parish Communion* (1937), which was arguably the greatest influence on the worshipping life of the Church of England during the middle decades of the twentieth century.[15]

It was undoubtedly this movement that helped restore the Eucharist to its central role within the life of the Church of England. This itself heralded the need for a proper return to liturgical study and liturgical reform. Following reports, then, on the place of the Book of Common Prayer and of saints in the Anglican tradition, a course was set fair for the future. The Church of England acted with wisdom in not *replacing* the Prayer Book with new rites, but maintaining instead that the Book of Common Prayer remains a key repository for Anglican theology, following the principle of *lex orandi, lex credendi*. Indeed, it was for this reason that its first collected book of revised liturgies was deliberately titled *The Alternative Service Book 1980*.

The first Liturgical Commission included a number of estimable scholars, namely Ronald Jasper, Geoffrey Willis, E. C. Ratcliff, Geoffrey Cuming, Colin Buchanan and Austin Farrer. The immediate output of the Commission was a set or series (as they were known) of experimental rites in separate booklets. Services from the 'deposited' Prayer Book of 1928 were authorized for use and published as Series I. The first entirely new rites in traditional language were titled Series II and the later set of liturgies in modern language became Series III. It would be an edited version of various of these

---

15 *They Shaped our Worship: Essays on Anglican Liturgists*, ed. Christopher Irvine (London: SPCK, 1998), p. 69. See also Christopher Irvine, *Worship, Church and Society: An Exposition of the Work of Arthur Gabriel Hebert to Mark the Centenary of the Society of the Sacred Mission (Kelham) of which he was a member* (Norwich: Canterbury Press, 1993).

that would be published as the one-volume Alternative Service Book in 1980. Twenty years later a very significantly revised set of liturgies was published as *Common Worship*. These liturgies were the beneficiaries of significant work completed between the publication of The Alternative Service Book and the entire corpus of new rites.[16] The final volume of *Common Worship* – Ordination Rites – was published in 2007. But still, the first set of revised rites was a remarkable achievement, although without unfairly deprecating the ASB, undoubtedly, *Common Worship* was a very significant advance on the earlier revision, and benefited from the most imaginative strands of the 'paradigm shift' outlined earlier. The supplementary volumes focusing on *Festivals* and *Times and Seasons* recovered much of the best traditional material, reaching back to the Patristic period, but it also included much entirely original work. Both the language of this new material and the choreography of the rites offered a richness, a variety and an imagination which has helped transform liturgical practice across the Church of England.

Concealed within all this, however, is one central irony. The new rites came together under the title *Common Worship*, but there is such a variety and permissiveness about their practical use that it has led some to describe the new volumes as a 'directory of worship' rather than a Book of Common Prayer. In a most interesting article written to celebrate the three hundred and fiftieth anniversary of the Book of Common Prayer, Paul Bradshaw adverts to the fact that this loss of common practice has a longer history than even the past half century. He points out that 'the first English Prayer Book of 1549 . . . [expressed the intention] . . . that "all the realm shall have but one use".'[17] Indeed the term Act of Uniformity was applied on each occasion that a new rite was

---

16 Cf. for example *Lent, Holy Week and Easter* (London: Church House Publishing, 1984); *The Promise of His Glory* (London: Church House Publishing, 1990); *Patterns for Worship* (London: Church House Publishing, 1989); *New Patterns for Worship* (London: Church House Publishing, 2002); *Enriching the Christian Year* (London: Church House Publishing, 1993).

17 Paul Bradshaw, 'Liturgical Development: From Common Prayer to Uncommon Worship', in *Comfortable Words: Polity, Piety and the Book of Common Prayer*, ed. Stephen Platten and Christopher Woods (London: SCM Press, 2012), p. 121.

produced in the sixteenth and seventeenth centuries. Bradshaw indicates how the politics of the Church of England pointed liturgical usage in multivarious directions, from very early on in the twentieth century, beginning with the ritualist controversy, then through the debates on the 1928 Prayer Book. So, after Parliament's rejection of the 1928 book, Bradshaw notes:

> The bishops themselves were partially responsible for encouraging the first of these (deviations) when in 1929 they put out the statement that 'during the present emergency and until further order be taken', they would not 'regard as inconsistent with loyalty to the principles of the Church of England the use of such additions or deviations' as fell within the limits of the 1928 proposals.[18]

Bradshaw concludes:

> there is much more to be said for a shared liturgical experience than is often heard nowadays, when the greater elasticity envisaged by the Letters of Business in 1906 seems to have been stretched to breaking point.[19]

This, then, is a salutary reminder that this paradigm shift is more radical than any previous revolution in liturgical development. It resonates with that fear expressed by Guéranger in the 1840s about liturgical variety. We are all the beneficiaries of a hitherto unknown liturgical imagination and variety. At the same time, however, in moving from church to church we may rarely encounter precisely the same liturgy. This is even true to some extent within the Roman Catholic Church with choice of eucharistic prayers and other variable material, but within that communion there remains a tightly drawn compass of doctrine expressed in the *Catechism* and mediated by the Magisterium. Anglicanism, which prides itself in the *lex orandi, lex credendi* approach to worship and belief, will increasingly find it more difficult to express

---

18 Bradshaw, 'Liturgical Development', pp. 126–7.
19 Bradshaw, 'Liturgical Development', p. 131.

an agreed doctrinal tradition, without careful reflection upon the kaleidoscopic nature of its liturgical rites.

Recovering a Sense of History

As we have already noted, there was a sense of renaissance as well as innovation within this liturgical revolution. Much historical liturgical scholarship was radical in its impact. Perhaps the shift to westward celebration of the Eucharist is the most potent example here.[20] The accretions of the Middle Ages (some of which bear a great richness in themselves) had obscured many of the theological origins of both the Eucharist and other sacraments. Some of the most interesting revivals and rediscoveries here relate to the rites of Christian initiation. The tradition of mystagogical catechesis, relating baptism and confirmation (seen as parts of one rite) to the Paschal mysteries is particularly vivid in its impact. The catechumens set out on Ash Wednesday to be catechized – trained like athletes – as they prepare for the glories but also the exigencies of Holy Week and Easter. The work of the Jesuit theologian Father Edward Yarnold SJ was very influential and powerful here,[21] inasmuch as he was a pioneer in rediscovering the power and practical impact of the early rites.

It was this specific area of research that helped give birth to the Roman Catholic Rite of Christian Initiation of Adults. This catechetical approach allows people (it has been adapted for children too) to join a group and gradually learn and be inducted into the key elements of Christian belief in their own time and at their

---

20 Interestingly enough, a certain element of liturgical fundamentalism crept in at this point. Every altar in every church and every chapel must become westward facing. It is clear, however, that some buildings are so designed to preclude anything other than an eastward celebration. Furthermore, there is a perfectly respectable theological *raison d'être* for such a practice as priest and people look forward, offering praise to the transcendent God, who in the glorified Christ is ever before us and interceding for us.

21 Edward Yarnold SJ, *The Awe-Inspiring Rites of Initiation* (Collegeville: Liturgical Press, 1971, 1994).

own rate. Hence, there can be a rolling pattern which is repeated and people may join and prepare for baptism and confirmation at different points along this continuous journey. Anglicans too have embraced the catechetical movement, and the so-called Pilgrim Course is influenced by this approach.[22] The catechetical approach allows for a *dramatic performance* of the sacraments. In a contemporary rite derived from the catechetical movement, as in the primitive Church, the preferred time for baptism is Easter and at the Paschal Vigil, and so at the heart of the Paschal mysteries. As catechumens (candidates) approach baptism, they are wearing their everyday clothes, albeit not over-clad. The priest either immerses them fully or they stand within a large font (as seen in the baptisteries of late antiquity). They are plunged three times into the water, in the name of Father, Son and Holy Spirit. They are 'drowned', that is, taken down into the tomb with Christ only to be raised with him. The neophytes (those just baptized) then change into an outfit entirely of pure white which symbolizes their new status within the resurrection life of the Church. Sometimes, if the church building is close to a river, there may indeed be an attempt to regain the resonances of Christ's own baptism in the Jordan, by John the Baptist, by total immersion in the river.[23]

The prodigious use of oil within the liturgy has equally been recovered and given new currency across all traditions within the Church. At baptism and confirmation the oil of catechumens and chrism are both used, and the oil of healing is used in the anointing of the sick. This usage has also brought the 'Mass of the Oils' on Maundy Thursday back into the mainstream Christian calendar. At this Eucharist, generally in the cathedral, the diocesan bishop blesses each of these three oils. At this same service deacons, priests and bishops also reaffirm their ordination vows and laity are encouraged to attend to emphasize the fullness of God's

---

22 *Pilgrim Course: A Course for the Christian Journey* (London: Church House Publishing, 2013).

23 The present author was indeed prevailed upon to baptize in the sea at Spittal, just south of Berwick-upon-Tweed, where the parish church is just 100 yards from the beach. Cf. *Berwick Advertiser*, 14 October 2016 and also Newcastle Diocesan Newspaper for October 2016.

Church. It is a profound moment in Holy Week, focusing on the priestly ministry of the Church.

This recovery of earlier patterns has been complemented by a similarly innovative approach to the seasons of Lent and Easter, Advent and Christmas. Within the Church of England, during the revision process, material was gathered together within two main volumes for these seasons.[24] These volumes have since become part of the library of liturgical material included within the wider heading of Common Worship. The increasing popularity of Advent carol processions and even Epiphany processions are another manifestation of this dual process of recovery and innovation. Throughout, a rich treasury of seasonal material is available for all feasts and special celebrations.

The Christian Journey

As we have already seen, with the advent of the Pilgrim Course, the image of the Christian life as a journey has become an increasingly important metaphor. It is a metaphor with a good pedigree even within the Church of England. In the confirmation rite of the Book of Common Prayer, the words used at the 'laying on of hands' capture the spirit of the Christian journey perfectly:

Defend, O Lord, this thy Child (or this thy Servant) with thy heavenly grace, that *he* may continue thine for ever; and daily increase in thy Holy Spirit, more and more, until *he* come unto thine everlasting Kingdom. Amen.

In the Common Worship rite this prayer remains, but is now said by everyone. In this way, it reminds all present that this rite is but one further episode along the road of the Christian life. Frequently now, more and more dioceses are including cathedral confirmation services

---

24 *Lent, Holy Week and Easter* (London: Church House Publishing, 1984) and *The Promise of His Glory* (London: Church House Publishing, 1990); *New Patterns for Worship* (London: Church House Publishing, 2002); *Enriching the Christian Year* (London: Church House Publishing, 1993).

which are themselves 'pilgrim', progressive or stational rites. There will be a progression from the font, the place of entry into God's Church, through to the place of the laying on of hands and finally to the place of communion, where the entire congregation is encouraged to move into the eastern part of the church (that part of the building where we often remember Christ's continuing intercession for all of us). They will receive communion standing and so they receive it 'in solidarity'. This reminds all that our creation and redemption is not an act of God purely of an individual nature, but instead places our communion within the redemption of all humanity through what New Testament theologians have sometimes described as the 'Christ-event'. Humanity is created and redeemed 'in solidarity'.

Pilgrimage itself has also become more popular within cathedrals. Their shrines are now often the focus or destination of the pilgrimage. Arrival in the cathedral is celebrated in a liturgical act as a *liminal* moment, a crossing of a new threshold and thus an opportunity for the renewal and deepening of a Christian's life and witness. St Cuthbert's shrine in Durham and the place of Thomas Becket's martyrdom in Canterbury Cathedral have become popular again as focuses of pilgrimage. So too the shrine at Walsingham remains a centre for pilgrimage. Often, specific commemorations of saints can offer a focus for this aspect of liturgical observance.[25] The *camino*, the road/route (or series of routes) to Santiago de Compostela, in north west Spain, is the most dramatic and populous of all pilgrim routes. Much literature is now available and even novels have captured the spirit of the journey.[26]

This recovery of pilgrimage and journeying is part of a wider and different aspect of the 'liturgical revolution' in the use of movement, space and gesture. So, there is now an encouragement in the baptism rite, for example, at the point where the candidate states 'I turn to Christ', to see the candidate physically turning in a new direction. It is during the Apostles' Creed (but not the Nicene)

---

25 One of the most extensive examples of this was Pilgrims' Way, in 1997, a celebration/commemoration of the arrival of St Augustine in Canterbury and the death of St Columba on Iona. Pilgrims travelled from Rome across to Canterbury and then four separate routes radiated from Canterbury, finally arriving in Derry, close to the birthplace of Columba.

26 See David Lodge, *Therapy* (London: Secker and Warburg, 1995).

that, again, a turning to the east indicates a turning to Christ in faith. The giving of a candle at baptism also offers an opportunity for candidates to retain a memory of their baptism and perhaps even light the candle annually on the anniversary of their baptism.

Similarly, in the ordination rite, there is now a careful choreography to indicate the drama of the ordinands' commitment at this moment of grace. So, deacons begin seated within the congregation at the start of the rite and are 'called' out from the wider congregation for this specific ministry. Priestly ordinations, in contrast, however, will begin with the deacons who are to be priested entering as part of the procession of clergy. The calling this time is to another order, but within the wider 'sacred ministry' of the Church. Sometimes ordinands will prostrate themselves (another example of recovering a practice from earlier patterns) as a sign of their offering. Often a chalice and paten are given to priests. Bishops receive their pastoral staffs from the archbishop or senior consecrator as they are ordained. Such symbolism enriches the drama of the rites.

Alongside the normal patterns within the parish, much of what has been described here relates directly to cathedrals and their ministry. This burgeoning of liturgical imagination has offered cathedrals, in particular, with their more plentiful resources, an enhanced opportunity to become centres of liturgical excellence, not, however, seizing a monopoly within a diocese, but instead allowing their resources to be of benefit to the Church more widely within both diocese and region. In a number of dioceses, liturgical committees convened by the cathedral precentor have encouraged parishes to bring candidates to cathedrals for a stational baptism and confirmation rite. Alternatively such training sessions have provided training sessions which have encouraged greater imagination within parish baptism and confirmation rites.

Occasional Offices

It is perhaps too rarely acknowledged just how formative the ministry of the Church of England (notably through the use of the Book of Common Prayer) has been upon English society. Certainly the marriage rite has had a significant impact on patterns of family life over a period of more than four hundred and fifty years.[27] With the increasing popularity of other venues, and notably secular buildings including hotels and stately homes, it would have been easy for the Church to lose its place in the proper formation of married life. For this reason, and because the Marriage Measure 2008 was also on the horizon, the Archbishops' Council, in 2007, set up the Weddings Project. The project saw the Church of England teaming up with a private research company to discover how those preparing to be married viewed the Church. The results enabled a teaching project to be rolled out across the Church to encourage clergy to set out more attractively the possibilities and benefits of marriage in church.[28] The Weddings Project was wide-ranging in its scope. It has helped both clergy and those preparing for marriage by indicating ease of access to the Church of England's marriage rites. First, both the practicalities of preparing for marriage and its symbolic/sacramental significance are covered and all this has been further consolidated on the Church of England's website. Second, there is a clear emphasis on preparing for the liturgy and music which will be used. Indeed, often, clergy use the marriage rite itself to structure their sessions on marriage preparation. Once again the innovative changes in attitudes to the liturgy are of great benefit in this process.

Still more recently a further project has been launched to offer similar support to clergy and laity both with regard to baptisms (frequently known as 'christening') and also funerals.[29] A very large proportion of funerals are still conducted by Church of England clergy simply by dint of establishment: everyone in England lives in an Anglican parish and has the right to request a church funeral. Similarly, all who so desire may ask for baptism for themselves or for their children if they live within a particular parish. The 'birth and death project' seeks to assist and encourage parish clergy in both these areas and, indeed, to give the laity of

---

27 Platten and Woods, *Comfortable Words*, especially chapter 1, pp. 1–19.
28 See www.yourchurchwedding.org
29 See www.churchgrowth.org

the parish proper and clear access to the rites of the Church. The renewal of liturgy increasingly offers opportunities for shaping a rite to convey both theological depth and pastoral care.

In dealing with families and other mourners in preparation for funerals, great care and sensitivity are an essential. There must therefore be clear, proper preparation in relation to the funeral rite, the music and the setting being offered to those who come. Increased resources, made available through liturgical renewal, allow still better opportunities here to offer comfort, care and, in the most subtle manner possible, some resources for interpreting the events and experience of all who are involved in funeral rites and requiems.

Missionary liturgy

Over the years, different keywords gain popular currency and this is as true in theology as it is in other disciplines. At one point, *ministry* was the focal term and in recent years the emphasis has moved to *mission*.[30] The shift is understandable in a climate that is not over-friendly to religion, Christianity and the Church. Certainly it is an imperative placed upon God's Church to pass on the gospel message as contemporary 'apostles'; the word *Mass* itself implies mission since it derives from the dismissal at the end of the Eucharist (the Latin dismissal is *ite, missa est*). We are dismissed to take the gospel to the wider world. Mission, however, is often seen rather narrowly and this has had its impact upon the resources and emphasis placed upon the liturgy. The appointment of a *Worship Development Officer* by the General Synod of the Church of England required much energy, debate and persuasion before the first appointment was made in 2005. In the three subsequent appointments the resources and proportion of hours allowed in the national church budget for this post have

---

30 For a moderate rant on this subject, see Stephen Platten, 'The Grammar of Ministry and Mission', *Theology*, 113:875 (September/October 2010), pp. 348–56.

successively been reduced. The assumption is that the liturgy is not missionary in nature or function. Although it is true that the offering of the liturgy, the *Opus Dei*, can never be utilitarian, since we worship through God's grace and as a natural response to God's gift in that grace, nevertheless the performance of the liturgy, if performed adequately, can effectively be a missionary act.

So much of what has been received through what we have described as the 'liturgical revolution', *the new paradigm*, has increased the missionary power of the liturgy. Early on in this essay we noted the Ulster priest who was moved to say that his experience of the Paschal Vigil was one of the most 'missionary' experiences in his Christian life. Similarly the use of pilgrimage/ stational liturgies for baptism and confirmation leaves with the baptisands/confirmands a memory that will never be erased. It deepens their perception of the gospel. The generous use of 'sprinkling' and the widening use of 'anointing' again speak powerfully of the sacraments. It would be otiose and tedious to repeat examples already given, but it is clear that, irrespective of style or churchmanship, liturgies well performed are as *missionary* as any other form of Christian witness. In a rather over-quoted aphorism, St Francis of Assisi is said to have challenged people, 'Preach the gospel on all occasions and where necessary use words.' The liturgy, by definition, does both these things.

A Tribute

If one were seeking out just one person to exemplify almost all that has been argued in this brief essay, one could hardly focus on a better example than Bishop Michael Perham. From theological college onwards, Michael manifested a passionate interest in the liturgy. It has been a passion, however, not born of prissiness, nor of a recondite and obscure obsession with history or form. Instead, Michael has applied his learning to the performance of the liturgy. In the contemporary Church, no one has been more prolific in publishing monographs and handbooks to assist in making liturgical performance more professional, more effective, more pastorally sensitive and so more *missionary*. From his early Alcuin book on *The Eucharist*, through to *A New Handbook of Pastoral Liturgy*,[31] and all that has followed, Michael has made good liturgical practice both accessible and exciting. It is not, however, only through published works that he has achieved his liturgical excellence. As a parish priest in Poole, as precentor of Norwich Cathedral, as Dean of Derby and then as Bishop of Gloucester, Michael has been an exemplar of all that he has written and given in countless courses and liturgies across the world. This essay is but one tiny attempt to summarize the liturgical revolution that has produced the new paradigm of which Michael is the very quintessence.

---

31 Michael Perham, *The Eucharist*, Alcuin Club (London: SPCK, 1978); Michael Perham, *A New Handbook of Pastoral Liturgy* (London: SPCK, 2000).

5

Making *Common Worship*: Securing Some Underlying Theologies

DAVID STANCLIFFE

When priests make the Declaration of Assent publicly before being licensed to any cure of souls, they rehearse their loyalty not only to the 'faith uniquely revealed in the Holy Scriptures and set forth in the catholic creeds', but to the Church of England's 'witness to Christian truth in its historic formularies, the Thirty-nine Articles of Religion, *The Book of Common Prayer* and the Ordering of Bishops, Priests and Deacons'.[1] Priests respond to the bishop's Preface in these words: 'I . . . declare my belief in the faith which is revealed in the Holy Scriptures and set forth in the catholic creeds and to which the historic formularies of the Church of England bear witness'; and significantly they conclude, 'and in public prayer and administration of the sacraments, I will use only the forms of service which are authorized or allowed by Canon'. This is why the texts used in worship are subjected to rigorous scrutiny not only in the House of Bishops, but though the laborious revision processes of the General Synod.

As there is no confessional statement or body of teaching in the Church of England remotely parallel to the corpus of papal pronouncements or the Augsburg Confession, we depend on liturgical formularies to hold our doctrine of the Church, its ministry and mission. Surprisingly, few of my episcopal colleagues take much interest in liturgy. Worship arouses strong feelings rather than theological engagement, and more than one bishop used the old chestnut: 'What's the difference between a terrorist and

---

1 *Common Worship; Services and Prayers for the Church of England* (London: Church House Publishing, 2001), p. xi.

a liturgist? You can negotiate with a terrorist!' to excuse their ignorance or disinterest (and get a laugh from the synod!) while revealing the natural conservatism of those whose foundations feel threatened in a way they can't quite pin down.

Since I believed that the texts used in worship had a significance beyond the ordering of worship, I said yes early in 1993 to the Archbishop of York's proposal that I should chair the Liturgical Commission. I had been very reluctant, as I had enjoyed being a working member on the Commission under the benign and droll, but fair-minded, Bishop Colin James (a gentleman rather than a player, to use his own cricketing distinction), but knew that access to the House of Bishops for the Chair of the Commission was essential to the success of the substantial revisions that would be needed before the 2000 deadline for the Alternative Service Book's replacement. John Habgood brushed aside my reservations, saying that he would make sure that I could have access to the House of Bishops whenever I needed it; within two months I found myself asked to be Bishop of Salisbury!

As its name implied, the ASB was designed as an alternative to the Book of Common Prayer, and its name, combined with a combative style of presentation, succeeded in polarizing not only regular worshippers but also the cultural battalions of England, including the Prince of Wales. The ASB 1980 had been authorized for an initial period of ten years, later extended to twenty, but by the early 1990s it was clear that the revision for the year 2000 needed to win back those who preferred the old, as well as developing the new. The continuing popularity of Choral Evensong, and the drawing power of Compline together with the BCP service of Holy Communion (without the long Exhortations) made them candidates for inclusion in a book which also contained the contemporary order of the Eucharist in the shape now well established ecumenically. It was the style and quality of language rather than the underlying theology and doctrine that seemed more central to people's concerns in the wider world, though in the world of the Synod the election process ensured plenty of members, especially lay members, with strongly held theological opinions. *Common Worship* was conceived therefore not so much as a compromise between the crusaders in different camps as an inclusive book that contained what was actually in regular use in both contemporary and traditional language, built round a core that was theologically sound and ecclesiologically coherent.[2]

Although Church House Publishing was keen to produce books, the volume of material and the need for churches to make pastorally informed choices led the Commission to prepare for digital publishing from the start. With much material available online, it was clear that the concept of a series of volumes, all accessible digitally, to complement the main *Common Worship* volume, was the only way to proceed.

Daily Prayer

Cranmer's ideal had been to have Morning and Evening Prayer said publicly in every church, with as many lay people as possible joining the parson. But busy lives and the individualization of personal prayer had meant that, even for clergy, the idea that we were bound together by taking part in the daily prayer of the Church, praying and so being formed by the same Scriptures and psalms, had been overtaken by more individualistic patterns such as a 'quiet time' or an individually tailored diet of what an individual found nourishing.

By the end of the 1980s, there was widely expressed dissatisfaction with the BCP's Morning and Evening Prayer as a pattern that could nourish clergy and lay people looking for a scripturally based diet for their daily prayer. Could we find a pattern that might unite people of very different habits around a more reflective use of the psalms, canticles and readings coupled with some degree of seasonal variation? The ASB provision had been little more than a version of Cranmer's amalgamated monastic offices in contemporary language, but by 1988 the Mirfield Father George Guiver had introduced a simpler, non-monastic style of daily prayer to a

---

2 See David Hebblethwaite, *Liturgical Revision in the Church of England 1984–2004: The Working of the Liturgical Commission*, Joint Liturgical Studies 57 (Cambridge: Grove Books, 2004), p. 23.

more general audience in his *Company of Voices*.[3] Many people had found in the Franciscan *daily office* book enrichment to the ASB pattern, and when the Franciscans signalled that they were thinking of a substantial revision, they were readily persuaded to prepare the drafts with a wider group. So Brother Tristam SSF (as the secretary, editor and chief factotum) and I drew together a group representing widely different traditions in order to test the appetite for something less monastic and more broadly appealing.

There was a real desire to find a new pattern to meet these needs, and the resulting convergence produced *Celebrating Common Prayer* in 1992, a version of *The Daily Office SSF* which the Franciscans published separately in brown with a central section of their own distinctive material, while the CCP version in blue astonished its publisher by selling 40,000 copies in its initial run! Brother Tristam and I produced some pocket versions for those travelling or pressed for time. This succeeded in uniting clergy and lay people over space and time in a pattern of regular prayer and was to form the basis of *Common Worship: Daily Prayer* (2005), now used probably by as many in its online form as from the book.

Initiation

Discipling and the rites of Christian initiation

The liturgical provision for rites round discipling and belonging raised important questions for the Church. Was the Church of England to become a close-knit group of firm believers with clear boundaries, or was it to retain – or recover – a vocation to be an inclusive body, with believers at different stages of their journey and low thresholds for enquirers? In the wider ecumenical context too, rites of initiation were at the forefront of discussion. How did people become disciples, and what rites at which stage should accompany them on the way to full, regular and active

---

3 George Guiver CR, *Company of Voices* (London: SPCK, 1988).

participation in the life of Christ's Church? Does God demand instant and absolute conversion of life in everyone, or do some who long for God find the way slow and tortuous, and need to travel at their own speed?

The central question was, how was baptism, and the liturgical expression of what God might be doing in it and through it, related to the whole mission of the Church in making disciples? In the journey of discipleship, were intellectual formation and the ability to articulate your faith coherently a necessary prerequisite for baptism? How could we celebrate with those who, though baptized in infancy and maybe confirmed in their teens, had come to a renewed and vibrant faith later in life? There had been debates in the General Synod in the late 1980s on the catechumenate, and in one of them I remember speaking after Gavin Reid, at that time running the London Mission, and finding myself agreeing with almost every word he said. Coming to faith was a gradual process, marked by stages, he said, and for most people that process took an average of four years to become embedded. Did the mantra that belonging leads to believing have wider currency than I had imagined?

To make some progress, a small working group was established with two members from the Board of Education, two from the Board of Mission and two (Michael Vaisey and myself) from the Liturgical Commission; we met for what was booked to be a week's hard arguing out of the different emphases we were expected to bring. But we surprised even ourselves in finding in our first review of the territory that we had an entirely common mind; so Michael drafted our report overnight and in the morning we agreed it and departed. This was published in 1995 as *On the Way: Towards an Integrated Approach to Christian Initiation.*[4]

A number of key elements in the process were identified:

- While the ecumenical agreement that baptism in water with the Trinitarian formula is valid and unrepeatable is foundational, the stages that lead up to it and that develop from it vary.

---

4 For the emergence of these patterns in the Church of England, see *On the Way: Towards an Integrated Approach to Christian Initiation* GS Misc 444 (London: Church House Publishing, 1995, 1998).

- God's calling of candidates, the proclamation of the divine initiative of grace, and the subsequent journey from welcome through a sense of belonging to believing are all stages on the journey.
- A formal renunciation of evil and turning to Christ, the light of the world, sets candidates on their way; the badge of faith, a defence against the powers of darkness, is the sign of the cross inscribed on the forehead of each candidate.
- Moving to the place of baptism, where prayer over the waters in the font rehearses the theology of baptism, precedes the corporate recitation of the Apostles' Creed where the Church's faith is shared; each candidate makes a personal assent to this before they are plunged beneath the waters.
- Emerging from the waters, the baptized may be clothed in white and are then anointed with chrism to show that they are God's viceroys – members of his royal, priestly people who are now entrusted with responsibility for the care of the world and its peoples.
- The baptized may have hands laid on them (if the bishop is presiding), before being given the kiss of peace and led to the altar for the liturgy of the Eucharist at which they receive the bread of life and the cup of salvation.
- Finally, they are blessed and sent out with a light lit from the Paschal Candle as a sign of their being sent out as part of the Church's apostolic *missio*. Like the first apostles on the day of Pentecost, they are to go out to cherish, challenge and change the world.[5]
- Particularly significant is the recovery of the 'post-baptismal catechesis' – sitting down after the liturgical celebration with those newly baptized and confirmed to work out with them what difference this makes and what they should do about it, ranging from the adoption of a rule of life to the proper evaluation of gifts and skills, and the testing of vocation in its widest sense.

---

5 This description of a contemporary baptism and confirmation rite is based on *Common Worship: Christian Initiation* (London: Church House Publishing, 2006). *Common Worship* is the collective title given to the volumes that make up the new liturgies and prayers of the Church of England from 2000 onwards.

Where did we stand with regard to the development of the initiation rites along these lines? First, there was the rediscovery of coming to faith as a process. Second, there has been a re-evaluation of the rites that accompany the different stages of the process and their theological significance. Third, baptism has been discovered to be fundamental to our Christian identity as those made in the image and likeness of God, and so to our calling to live out the faith we profess.[6]

Taking the hospitality offered to enquirers seriously and accompanying adults on their journey into faith has a transforming effect on the life of the local church. The wholehearted celebration of each stage in this process has the power to change not only the lives of individual candidates but of communities that take the whole process of discipling seriously. It refocuses a community on the Church's mission – a mission which is less about 'taking the gospel' to people, as if we were the sole custodians of God's grace, and more about discovering what it is that God is doing in his world, helping people to recognize it, celebrate it and then take responsibility for ensuring that it happens.

Historic strands in baptismal theology

So what kind of ecclesiology do patterns like these imply? In the theology of baptism, two different historic strands are present. There is the *anamnetic* pattern – recalling Christ's dying and rising vividly by submerging the candidate in the watery tomb. Here, the sense of being called out of darkness into the light of Christ fits well with a Pauline theology of dying to sin and rising to new life, with the implication that baptism marks a sharp transition from the old life to the new. The imagery here is decisively Paschal, where the key biblical text (Romans 6.3–11) is read as the Epistle at the Paschal Liturgy. Fonts are large pools, if not flowing rivers,

---

6 These stages are laid out clearly in the RCIA, the *Rite of Christian Initiation of Adults* (study edition, Chicago: LTP, 1988), a programme developed to help Roman Catholic churches to recover the corporate celebration of baptism in communities.

and a literal submersion – a real drowning – gives the candidates that sense of totality they often long for. This pattern has often been assumed to be the early Church's norm, along with its accompanying expectation of instant conversion and total belonging aboard the ark of salvation. It provides a model of church with firm boundaries that is essentially *contra mundum*, sharply differentiated from the surrounding chaos, and offers instant salvation.

The other, an *epicletic* pattern, is founded more on a Johannine theology of a new birth by water and the Spirit. Here the experience of new disciples is less one of sudden conversion than of growing and deepening conviction. John's Gospel presents his Passion narrative as the reversal of the events of Genesis to establish the new creation, in which the Spirit who descends on Jesus as he emerges from the waters of the Jordan declares him to be both the one who will suffer for the people and the anointed Son. The key biblical text is John 3.1–17, Jesus' dialogue with Nicodemus about being born again by water and the Spirit, which links rising from the waters with being anointed for an approaching ministry. This Spirit-led growth into full maturity is a model that has analogies with natural human development.

This model of baptism suggests a theology of the Church as a new Israel, a pilgrim people on the way, rather than a fully fledged and radically distinct entity. The pattern is one of organic development and the Church is seen less as the ark of faith and more as the leaven in the lump. The central vocation of the believer is to be drawn into the life of the Trinity, experienced as living in a network of self-giving, loving relationships. In this model, the Church has softer boundaries and only gradually places more disciplined demands on the new Christian as they grow into faith, consciously welcoming those who don't want to risk putting more than a toe in the water to test the temperature, and letting them go at their own pace.

Managing multiple ecclesiologies

What was important for the Commission's rethink was to balance these two apparently conflicting ecclesiologies. Some in the

Church are more comfortable with the former, more black and white picture. For others, a church with sharp boundaries and clear discipline contradicts their image of the Christ who eats with tax-collectors and sinners; for these, a greater emphasis on the incarnational element of the faith, at any rate as a first stage, seems truer to the gospel of mercy. There are dangers in an either/or approach, which is what Cyril of Jerusalem avoids, as he reflects in his post-baptismal catechesis:

> When you went down into the water, it was like night, and you could see nothing. But when you came up again it was like finding yourself in the day. That one moment was your death and your birth; that saving water was both your grave and your mother.[7]

While these different emphases are best understood as complementary rather than mutually exclusive, it was a desire to move to a more inclusive model of the Church that prompted the Commission to provide a wider theological basis to the initiation rites in the period leading up to 2000. So 'Faith is the gift of God to his people' was a hard-won opening to the initiation rites, to make it clear that faith was not a personal achievement that would entitle you to baptism, but was part of what God was offering to the seeker.

The restoration and renewal of baptismal life

Another thread was the exploration of the commonest imperative in the New Testament: *metanoeite*, traditionally translated as 'Repent', with its connotations of wayside pulpits and fingers wagging at sexual peccadilloes.

In the context of initiation, *metanoeite* rather bears the meaning of 'change your direction' or 'get a life' in the way that teenagers

---

7 Cyril of Jerusalem, *Mystagogical Catecheses* II.4; these words are inscribed round the rim of the substantial cruciform baptismal font in Portsmouth Cathedral.

use the expression. Reflection here led us to consider continuous turning – what St Paul describes as dying daily to sin as you try constantly to tune the compass of your life to God's bearings. The processes of growth are gradual and largely hidden.

These considerations led us to see that the penitential rites that celebrate restoration of the baptismal status as well as services of wholeness and healing could be given a theologically coherent context by being placed in the same volume that drew together not just the rites about enquiry, discipling and belonging round baptism and confirmation, but also the rites marking the restoration of that baptismal gift – the ever-present assurance of God's mercy and forgiveness – in rites of reconciliation and renewal.

Rites of Ordination

One of the reasons why the Ordinal is important is that this is where one can find the Church of England's theology of the distinctive orders of ministry clarified. *Saepius Officio*, the formal response of the Archbishops of Canterbury and York to the Papal Bull of 1896, *Apostolicae Curae*, declaring Anglican orders to be 'absolutely null and utterly void', was drafted by my predecessor as Bishop of Salisbury, John Wordsworth. His robust defence of what the Church of England thinks it has always been doing as well as saying in the rites of ordination is important for any reconciliation of ministries in the future.

At my episcopal ordination I had taken care to invite a bishop from the Old Catholic Church to take a full part lest the validity of my orders should ever be in question. But at the present, focusing on the recognition of ministries rather than the more limited concept of the validity of orders may help to find some common ground. Since Pope Paul VI's gift of his ring to Archbishop Michael Ramsey in 1966 (reaffirmed by Pope Francis's gift of a pastoral staff to Archbishop Justin Welby in 2016), what the Roman Catholic Church does and what it says have been recognizably at variance, and I was concerned to ensure the Church of England should have an ordination rite that could never again be called deficient!

As well as considering what an ordination does, it is important to consider what it says about the Church and its theology of ministry. Is an ordination like a graduation ceremony or a rite of installation – a public recognition of something that has happened? Or does something take place to alter the relationship between the ordinand and the Church?

When the House of Bishops was beginning to look at the revision of the Ordinal, I felt that the House might do well to think through some of the issues around not just what an ordination did but what it expressed, before we got down to the liturgical texts. Central to what I hoped they would grapple with was a theology of the three orders, since the distinctive nature of diaconal ministry had begun to be recovered from its being seen as little more than a probationary period before ordination to the priesthood.[8]

Ordinations are occasions where the ordering of the Church's common life is made visible. The ordination rite gives shape and order to the life of the whole Church of God. That community of faith is called to continue the work of Christ: it is into his body that we are baptized and thus empowered by the Spirit to become God's agent and instrument in bringing about his new creation. It is Christ's ministry that we share, and as Christ is the head of that body (Ephesians 4.15, 16), so the ordained ministry represents the ministry of Christ as Head of the body. There is a distinctive responsibility within the *laos* for the *klēros*. (2 Peter 5.3)

Although it can look as if the bishop is setting one or more of the people of God apart from the community of faith and transmitting to them a distinct power, the way in which the rite is celebrated makes it clear that ordination is the act of the whole community, presided over by the bishop, that not only publicly authorizes a particular member of the community of the baptized to bear a representative responsibility, but also constitutes the Church as the ordered expression of the divine life. So care has to be taken in text and symbol, as well as in presentation, not only to uphold the common baptismal foundation of all Christian

---

8 A report for ACCM in 1974, chaired by the Bishop of Newcastle, actually proposed the abolition of the diaconate in the Church of England, but was not accepted.

ministry, but also to clarify the distinctiveness of those called to and authorized as ministers in the historic orders.

The call of all the baptized is made clear at the start of the rite. We are to follow Christ, to be made corporately into a royal priesthood so that we may 'declare the wonderful deeds of him who has called us'. The whole Church is to witness to God's love and to work for the coming of his Kingdom. Those standing before the assembly are to be ordained into this distinctive order to serve this royal priesthood. While all the baptized are called to exercise their gifts in their discipleship, not all are called to be public, representative ministers.[9]

So what is distinctive about ordained ministry? There is only one ministry, and that is Christ's. Ordination as a minister makes visible in a particular person a distinctive call to Christ's ministry in his Church. Ordination places a person within that catholic order and is not primarily concerned with the way in which that ministry will be exercised locally. It is the needs of a given context – whether parish or chaplaincy – that will form the way in which that universal diaconate or priesthood is exercisedthere.

It is the task of an ordination rite, therefore, to make clear in one liturgical act the particular focus of the ministry to which the candidate is called. As in other rites, such as the funeral or marriage services, this liturgical rehearsal of a series of stages in a candidate's development in response to God's call is articulated by the rite: by the candidates' presentation, by their public examination and the assembly's assent to their ordination, by their visibly exercising the formal responsibilities of the ministry into which they have been ordained, by being equipped with the distinctive symbols of office, and by returning the candidates, authorized and acknowledged, to the particular communities in which they will exercise that universal ministry. This is how the Church makes clear that the candidate has a particular authority to minister in Christ's name within the body as a whole. But in the ordination rite, the emphasis is on what God in Christ has done

---

9 John N. Collins, *Are All Christians Ministers? A Different Answer to the Modern Question in the Churches* (Newtown, N.S.W.: E. J. Dyer (Australia) Pty Ltd, 1992).

and continues to do rather than on the particular people being ordained and their diverse gifts.

Towards a distinctive theology of each order

Ordination therefore does more than articulate publicly what the Church is doing. In an ordination it is God who empowers his people and orders his Church. The ministry in which we share is Christ's, and the sign of the candidates' incorporation into Christ's whole ministry that is common to all ordinations is prayer with the laying on of hands.

A clear theology of the distinctive nature of each order rather than a focus on functionality is important. A lack of a clearly articulated theology of orders results in too many people in the Church of England thinking that the three orders are bishops, vicars and curates (or sometimes bishops, ministers and readers!) with function and hierarchy as the basis of the distinction.

The right place to start, I believe, is with the work of Christ himself. Here is a simple matrix. God in Christ does two things for his people: first he shares our life, then he changes it. This is the heart of the faith, and it is then the Church's task to draw God's people into this process of engagement and transformation and to ensure that the pattern is absorbed, practised and handed on.

While this paradigm of the relationship between incarnation and redemption provides a model for how to structure a pastoral visit (listen first, and then decide what to offer or how to change things) or how to construct a liturgy (challenged by the ministry of the word to expect transformation in the celebration of the sacrament), in this context the paradigm is most significant as a means of teasing out the distinctive ministries of deacon, priest and bishop.

The diaconate focuses God's direct and personal engagement with us, his sharing our nature in Christ's incarnation, his being rooted in the particularity of time and place. This opens the door to a ministry of attention, service and the brokering that goes with the concept of Christ as the 'agent' of God. If Christ is the 'deacon of God',[10] then the deacon is one who is commissioned to undertake a specific task or deliver a specific message. At the heart of this incarnational ministry therefore are the twin categories of embassy and hospitality.

The priesthood focuses what St Paul describes as 'the upward call of God in Christ Jesus' (Philippians 3.14), the reconciling, redemptive action of Christ's perfect self-offering on the cross. This sacrificial movement of response to a God who 'calls us out of darkness into his marvellous light' sets redemptive change at the heart of the sacramental ministry of the priesthood. Movement and change are central to the paradigm of a missionary priesthood, but never at the expense of that unity with one another and with Christ and the one sacrifice offered at the one altar.[11]

Episcopal ministry embraces both diaconal and priestly ministry, but its distinctive focus of this apostolic and prophetic ministry is pastoral oversight. The mission of the twelve, and of the seventy, inaugurates the distinctive Pentecostal mission of the Church. This apostolic ministry enrols God's people in this process of engagement and transformation, and makes sure that this pattern is handed on. That is why episcopal ministry is focused liturgically in those occasions like baptism, ordination and the ratifying of initiation in confirmation. Those are celebrations where baptized Christians tumble to it that that is what they are, and begin to take adult responsibility for sharing in the Church's apostolic mission and ministry and its prophetic witness. It is here that the bishop's ministry as the focus of unity and the agent of communion with other parts of the Church is given expression in the ministry of pastoral oversight.

None of this means that bishops are the only ministers engaged in the Pentecostal task: it is clearly shared with other ministers and with the priestly people of God. But it is the bishops' responsibility to see that the Church is Pentecostal and apostolic, engaged in holding together the diversity of gifts in a way that builds up the

---

10 See Ignatius, Trall. 3.1 (https://www.ccel.org/ccel/richardson/fathers.vi.ii.iii.iii.html) and Mark 10.45.

11 See Ignatius, Magn. 7 (http://www.ccel.org/ccel/schaff/anf01.v.iii.vii.html).

body in its witness to the world. Nor is this is all that the bishops do. It is the bishops' responsibility to see that the whole Church is engaged in that process too, and to lead the Church out from the safety of the sheepfold to engage in its mission to everyone.

This sense of overlap is true of the other orders too. The diaconate is not an inferior order, where deacons never find themselves engaged in distinctively priestly or apostolic tasks: it is simply that the diaconate has a prime responsibility to remind the whole Church to engage with reality first, before attempting to transform – or more properly, to let God have the opportunity to transform – our lives. Diaconal ministry undergirds everything else, and all priests and bishops need to have this held constantly before them. As Gregory Nazianzus said, 'That which God did not assume, he did not redeem.'[12] Just as there can be no redemption without incarnation, so priests and bishops who have no diaconal foundation to their ministry are at risk of offering a ministry that has no point of engagement, but moves directly into the mode of redemptive change.

Expressing the distinctive nature of the order in each ordination rite

The basic rite of ordination is the laying on of hands with prayer within a celebration of the Eucharist, but there are a number of points at which the distinctive focus of each order can be expressed. The first is in the Presentation. Traditionally, it has been the archdeacon who has presented candidates, but would there not be more sense in someone who has had a hand in their formation presenting candidates for ordination to the diaconate? For candidates for the priesthood the most obvious person is probably the training incumbent and for the episcopate, the Crown's formal presentation might well be best exercised for suffragans by the diocesan bishop involved in their nomination and for diocesans a member of the Crown Appointments Commission.

---

12 Gregory Nazianzus, *Epistola* 101.7; cf. Athanasius, *De Incarnatione* 54.

A second element is clearly the Readings. Readings for the distinctive ministry of the priest, like those which focus on the ministry of reconciliation, for example, are out of place for the ordination of a deacon.

The Charge is a significant element in the Anglican tradition. It is one of the places, together with the ordination prayer itself and the collect and post-communion prayer, where the theology of each order is articulated. The Charge to priests in the Book of Common Prayer has been very significant in shaping our theology of priestly ministry over the centuries, and many priests know it by heart and return to it regularly for self-examination on the anniversary of their ordination. But there was never a Charge of comparable weight for the ordination of deacons. With renewed interest in the diaconate as an equal and independent order, *Common Worship* has introduced a longer Charge with more theological weight.[13] Revision of the Prayer Book's priestly and episcopal Charges acknowledged the growing significance of collaborative styles of working which required significant modification of the dominant sheep–shepherd model.

At the heart of each rite, the whole assembly is called to pray for the coming of the Holy Spirit, and engages in a litany. The presidential prayer that follows includes a preface-type thanksgiving to God for the gifts he has given and for calling the candidates and has at its heart an epicletic formula, repeated in the Anglican tradition with the simultaneous laying on of hands over each candidate (if there is more than one). The prayer concludes with intercession and a doxology, sealed with a great Amen. Priests join the presiding bishop in the laying on of hands when the ordination is to the priesthood (as bishops join the archbishop for the episcopate). Care needs to be taken that the laying on of hands does not interrupt the sense of the complete prayer overmuch: in some places the assembly's continuing prayer has been sustained by a murmured chant invoking the Holy Spirit.

---

13 Draft versions of a distinctively diaconal Charge were found particularly helpful at ordinations where the candidates were for the 'permanent' diaconate, though now all deacons benefit from a more robust theology of the diaconate than that offered in the BCP or ASB. HB(01)22, paras 156–8, comments on the ASB Charge.

A fifth element relates to the handing over of distinctive symbols to the newly ordained to symbolize their order. In the 1550 *Form and manner of making and consecrating Archebisshoppes, Bishoppes, Priestes and Deacons* and subsequent Ordinals, giving a copy of the New Testament took the place of the handing over of the Book of the Gospels to deacons and a copy of the Bible in place of the chalice and paten to priests. In the ASB, the possibility of giving the chalice and paten to priests and the pastoral staff to bishops in addition to the Bible was restored.

The only matter that provoked any opposition was the suggestion that the presentation of these 'tools for the trade', such as a bishop's pastoral staff or individual copies of the Bible, might be transferred to the end or sending out. With all ordinations now coming after the Gospel and sermon, distributing personal copies of the New Testament at this point to newly ordained deacons did not make much sense. What are they to do with them? The same was true of the handing over of the pastoral staff to newly consecrated bishops.

And what are newly ordained priests and bishops supposed to do with a Bible at this point in the service, when the Liturgy of the Word has just ended? If the Bible is to be given at this point, we argued, ought it not to be The Bible, the large lectern Bible which is handed to each candidate in turn, rather than the distribution of a mound of individual copies, which are best given at the end.

If anything beyond the ordination prayer and the laying on of hands is required at the central point in the rite, we suggested some visual underlining that might explicate the distinctive focus of each order, which of course would be optional.

For deacons, the custom of the bishop divesting himself of his vestments, tying a towel round his waist and washing the newly ordained deacons' feet has commended itself as a visible sign of the way in which a new deacon's ministry should be exercised and has made visible the relationship between the deacon and their bishop. Such a practice – originally an independent rite separate from the Eucharist of the Last Supper on Maundy Thursday, where it is now most commonly celebrated – roots the deacon's ministry in the gospel and helps to make sense of diaconal ministry to many in the congregation, especially to those who are not regular churchgoers. No words are said, but a chant such as

'Ubi Caritas' is sung, and if John 13.1–11 has been read as the Gospel, the deacon may finish the passage (John 13.12–20) after the bishop has vested again. After the exchange of the Peace, the newly ordained deacons can begin to give liturgical expression to the ministry to which they have been ordained by laying the Holy Table and preparing the gifts, and then taking part in the distribution of communion.

For priests, there is the posture of candidates during the Veni Creator and the litany. A telling symbol of the self-surrender of the candidates before the majesty of God as they place themselves at his disposal is to prostrate themselves flat on the floor. Candidates who have experienced this speak of its power – and it conveys their dependence on God vividly for the assembly.

The distinctive Gospel for priests (John 20.19–23) speaks of the risen Christ breathing over his apostles. (This visible handing over of the Spirit was given literal illustration in the Coptic Church where the Patriarch would breathe into a bladder that would be taken to the ordination and burst over the head of the candidate!) The Western tradition offers a symbol which is more readily recognizable as embodying the outpouring of the Holy Spirit, and links ordination to its roots in baptism: the anointing of the newly ordained, and specially this time the hands that are to bless and absolve. Though such symbolic acts are secondary, they may speak powerfully to people in the assembly of the outpouring of God's grace on those who have been chosen and appointed to hold the priestly ministry of Christ before his Church and given authority to preside at the celebration of the sacraments.

And the newly ordained – perhaps priests and bishops even more than deacons, with their traditional relationship with the bishop – need some kind of welcome into their respective orders. This says something important about entering a catholic order, whether diaconal, priestly or episcopal, and makes it clear that the newly ordained minister has a responsibility to and in the whole Church, not just to the local community. It certainly looks very odd to see the newly ordained returning to the seats they occupied as a candidate, as if the ordination had made no difference to how the Church was ordered. The time for returning people to their local church, whether this is bishops to the people of their dioceses or priests to the people of their parishes, is at the end of the service, as part of an extended dismissal rite where a representative – a churchwarden for priests or a lay chair or Lord Lieutenant for bishops – might lead them out.

Ordination can be a powerful sign to the very parochial parish that the Church's priestly ministry is not primarily about serving their needs – that is an essentially diaconal task – but about linking that cell of the Church's life with the universal priesthood of the Church and drawing them into that one perfect self-offering of the Son to the Father. But that universal ministry needs constantly to be re-earthed in the local, the particular – in fact the parochial. So the way in which priests (or bishops) are given back to their people is important. It may not require any words, like many of these signs, but the significance of the bishop handing back priests who have just been ordained to their training incumbent and members of their parish should not be underestimated.

It is important that people are not led to think that the only place in which the newly ordained priests or bishops can exercise their ministry is in their own local parish or diocese. When the bishop (or archbishop) invites the newly ordained priest(s) (or bishop(s)) to stand alongside them at the altar during the eucharistic prayer, vested according to their order, this sends out a powerful signal about the way in which collegiality is modelled. Of course the ordaining bishop can ignore the newly ordained, send them back to sit in the seats where they sat as candidates and continue with the eucharistic celebration as if there was no need of them. Strictly speaking, the bishop does not need them. But is that the signal it is intended to convey, or would a more inclusive gesture say something richer about the nature of the Church and the collegial nature of priestly and episcopal ministry that the newly ordained now share with the bishop?

Conclusion

What do I draw from this extended reflection on three of the many issues with which the Commission grappled? First, that there is an implicit ecclesiology – an often subliminally imparted teaching about the nature of the Church and its mission – in any rite. Second, that in order to chart the development of doctrine, we need to be more aware of the implicit teaching in our liturgical formularies. Third, while the rubrics in a rite are as subject to the Synod's authorization as the text, the Synod has never sought to try to control how the rites are celebrated. It is in this area that the Commission's responsibility in commending a style, and giving 'coaching hints' in a preface or a parallel publication, can be enormously significant. For many regular as well as more occasional worshippers, *how* the rites are celebrated is what develops habits that spill over from worship in church into how they behave corporately in the communities in which they are set.

6

'Be born in our hearts': Being Transported and Transformed by the Liturgy

TOM CLAMMER

Introduction

Praying transports us. Praying together in community, praying common words in particular locations, accompanied by distinctive rituals, transports us in particular ways, for it is a way of praying that is liturgical. Sometimes exposure to the liturgy is deliberate, for example in choosing to attend church on a Sunday week by week, perhaps in a particular place with a particular style which appeals to us. Sometimes liturgical prayer takes us by surprise, however. Sometimes we can be surprised by an encounter with the divine in a place, or at a time, or in a context which we were not expecting. The Church of England, with its distinctive parochial structure and its continued dedication to the occasional offices, combined with the innovations of pioneer ministry and fresh expressions, recognizes that the worship which is offered in public contexts, that which we describe as liturgy, is as varied and various as are the worshippers who engage with it. It recognizes also that, for some people, sustained engagement with, for example, the Eucharist, over months, years and even decades can be the place where the mind and soul are surprised by the presence of God, but surprisingly an encounter might just as easily take place in one's first immersion in liturgical prayer. Praying liturgically transports us.

I can't recall the moment I originally heard the first liturgical prayer I ever committed to memory. One of the few things that

seems to come naturally to me in ministry is the ability to memo-
rize huge sections of the liturgy. This almost photographic memory seems restricted to liturgical texts, as I almost never know
where my car keys are. However, during my years as a practising
Christian I have found that the words, and indeed the gestures, of
Anglican liturgical prayer have worked their way inside me and
a great number of them bubble to the surface whether bidden
or not. I know what the first liturgical text I ever memorized is
because it is a text which I use regularly to this day. It is one of the
short collects associated with the lighting of the Advent wreath:

> Lord Jesus, Light of the World,
> born in David's city of Bethlehem,
> born like him to be a king,
> be born in our hearts this Christmastide,
> be king of our lives today. Amen.[1]

I don't know what it is about this particular prayer that resonates with me. There is certainly something to do with the
cadence and rhythm of its construction, something to do with its
simplicity and the repetitive use of the word 'born' and 'king'.
I suspect also, however, that it was the context in which the
prayer was used that helped it to lodge in that bit of my mind
and heart which was developing a liturgical awareness and
amassing a set of prayer resources that were going to sustain
my life as a young Christian. I think I heard it first as a teenager
in the little rural parish church in which I was worshipping, and
in which I was encountering for the first time this extraordinary
thing called liturgy, this 'subtle blend of word, song, movement,
gesture and silence that enables the people of God to worship
together'.[2] I have vivid memories of my first and second Advents
as a churchgoing Christian in that place: I can recall the Advent
wreath, the light of the winter sun through the rather stylized

---

1 *The Promise of His Glory: Services and Prayers for the Season from All
Saints to Candlemas* (London: Church House Publishing, 1994), p. 137.

2 M. Perham, *New Handbook of Pastoral Liturgy* (London: SPCK, 2000),
p. 3.

Victorian stained glass, the deep purple of the vicar's advent stole, and some of the words we said and sang which heralded this new world into which I was being drawn. I remember the introductory sentence set in the Alternative Service Book for Advent Sunday, 'Now it is time to awake out of sleep, for now our salvation is nearer than when we first believed.'[3] I remember also that collect. I know I have prayed it out loud every year since the year 2000 which is as far back as my archive of sermons takes me, and I believe I used it much earlier than that. I didn't know until quite recently that the prayer was composed by Michael Perham, and first appeared in *The Promise of His Glory* where it is simply attributed to St George's, Oakdale, before being included in *Common Worship: Times and Seasons* upon its publication.[4] Since that early encounter with liturgy in what seemed at the time a desperately exciting and intriguing new world, liturgy has continued to inhabit me as I inhabit it. It has transported me on numerous occasions and caused a very profound change in me, and I carry that particular collect with a special thanksgiving.

In this essay I would like to explore the way in which the liturgy transports us. I will do so through the lens of the liturgical theology of David Fagerberg, which I have found particularly helpful in my own journey. I will do so through a brief examination of the Church of England's own liturgical theology, then through a discussion of the way in which context shapes the way in which liturgy is performed. I will use examples from both rural parochial ministry and the ministry of cathedrals to illustrate ways in which liturgy can be created that has the potential to transport both the regular worshipper and the person who stumbles upon liturgy unawares. I will recognize the challenges which confront those trying to create liturgy that transports, particularly the challenges associated with rural ministry. In concluding I will return to the parish church in which I first heard the Advent wreath collect, and

---

3 *Alternative Service Book 1980* (London: SPCK, 1980), p. 422.
4 *Common Worship: Times and Seasons* (London: Church House Publishing, 2006), p. 51.

I will argue that attention to the practicalities of liturgical performance is in fact a principle of liturgical preparation.

Doing Liturgical Theology

There is of course an almost endless variety of liturgical contexts. My ministry thus far has enabled me to engage in suburban, rural and cathedral settings for both regular and occasional worship, and I shall draw on those later. There are almost endless varieties of worshippers: the tiny rural congregations at 8 o'clock communion services in January, huge civic funeral congregations, the eager and slightly alarmed bride and groom on their wedding day, surrounded by ushers and bridesmaids representing their school and university friends, midday prayers in a cathedral teeming with visitors on a sunny Saturday in August, and those extraordinary crematorium congregations, perhaps made up of only four or five elderly people plus the vicar and the bearers, bidding farewell to a friend, a life companion, in her 97th year. In all of these and a thousand other contexts the liturgy, when alive through its utterance by minister and people, by its contextualization in a particular place, with particular music, movement and intention, opens the door to a bigger world in which questions can be asked, hopes and fears aired, and the hints of heaven perceived.

The liturgy has to be prayed for this to work. Just as a play is supposed to be acted and needs an audience, so the liturgy is supposed to be prayed and needs a congregation. The Church of England has always been uneasy at the prospect of trying to define in concrete terms what it believes is happening in its liturgy. There are places, however, where we find direction. In the preface to the Declaration of Assent the 'historic formularies' of the Church of England are afforded the status of expounders or defenders of doctrine. This makes it clear that the Church of England believes that the words it uses matter because they tell us something about what it is that we believe. The Declaration of Assent refers to public liturgy among the historic formularies – the Thirty-Nine Articles of Religion, the Book of Common Prayer, and the Ordering of Bishops, Priests and Deacons – as being the texts which 'bear witness' to the faith which is 'revealed in the Holy Scriptures and set forth in the catholic creeds'.[5] How and what we pray matters because our praying witnesses to our believing. Thus something approaching the *lex orandi, lex credendi* model, the conviction that the 'law of praying' is, or demonstrates, the 'law of believing', appears to be operating in the Church of England. Liturgical theologians such as David Fagerberg argue that the only true venue and context for liturgical theology is the liturgical arena itself. Liturgical theology cannot exist as an academic discipline distinct from a community at worship. As Fagerberg puts it, 'the subject matter of liturgical theology is not liturgy, it is God, humanity and the world, and the vortex in which these three existentially entangle is liturgy'.[6]

If liturgy is the curious and wonderful intersection of the divine, the world and human experience that produces something called 'liturgical theology', which is not an academic discipline but the reality and 'guts' of a people doing their thinking about what the relationship between God and themselves might be, then all liturgy has the potential to surprise us and transport us. No one can ever know what might be revealed about the relationship between God, humanity and the world in any liturgical occasion, and that revelation might at any given point feel comforting, challenging, provocative or even laced with judgement as broken humanity and the broken world encounter the unchanging and faithful God of love.

Being taken by surprise

There is, however, something about the chance, brief or unexpected encounter with liturgy which seems to be particularly curious, transformative and wonderful. It is encountered, for example, in cathedrals. I hear testimony of this regularly as I bid farewell to visiting worshippers after Choral Evensong. The ministry

---

5 *Common Worship: Services and Prayers for the Church of England* (London: Church House Publishing, 2000), p. xi.

6 D. W. Fagerberg, *What is Liturgical Theology?* (Collegeville: Liturgical Press, 1992), p. 10.

of shaking hands, which my colleagues and I sometimes rather uncharitably refer to as the 'grip and grin', reveals the degree of surprise with which very similar stories are told to the Canon in Residence about the way in which choral worship has 'taken me somewhere I didn't expect to go'. These regular testimonies are a useful reminder that one does not have to understand the grammar or vocabulary of the liturgy, or have a comprehensive knowledge of its history and development, for it to do its work. Study of, and familiarity with, the liturgy is good and interesting, but entirely non-essential. There is a similar thing going on when the visitor encounters, accidentally, a Eucharist happening in a side chapel which they had only popped into to examine the reredos, and ends up sitting quietly at the back throughout and experiences for the first time, or maybe finds familiar words and phrases welling up from a repository they forgot that they possessed, the story of a body broken and of blood shed, and the assertion that 'Christ died for you'.[7] Those who minister in cathedrals experience this liturgical theology, in Fagerberg's sense of the word, perhaps particularly visibly, and we tend to talk about it a lot, but it happens in parish churches too, and indeed as the opening paragraphs of this essay describe, it was in a parish church that it first happened to me when I had not a clue about the symbol system, and found the vocabulary entirely alien.

These encounters, these coincidences of the world, humanity and God, are not only the purpose of liturgy, they *are* liturgy. The work to which the Church is called is worship. It is our highest and our primary calling. It is the proper co-operation with the operation of the Holy Spirit within the life of the world to which men, women and children alike are called through baptism, responding in prayer to that faith which is 'the gift of God to his people'.[8] Of course the Holy Spirit moves mightily and mysteriously whether or not God's people happen to be praying together at the time, but liturgical encounters by their nature are spaces within the temporal and material world where the life of heaven

---

7 Invitation to communion, *Common Worship* (2000), p. 180.

8 *Common Worship: Christian Initiation* (London: Church House Publishing, 2006), p. 66.

breaks in with glory and grace, and some of that has to do with how we pray and what we pray. These are those moments and occasions where it is as if, as the hymn writer puts it:

... man, the marvel seeing, forgets his selfish being, for joy of beauty not his own.[9]

To be captivated by the 'joy of beauty not our own', to be swept up with the angels and archangels, or indeed just as much to become aware of our need for repentance, or forgiveness, has much to do with the work of the Holy Spirit, but these opportunities can be made the more accessible, or indeed less so, by the ministry of the Church. If the calling of the Church in its public worship is to nothing else, it is to do our best not to get in God's way, to at least be open to the possibility that in every act of liturgical worship the Kingdom of God might be glimpsed. Almost twenty years ago Michael Perham accused the Church of forgetting this most fundamental of its callings:

> I am not worried that we fail to find ourselves caught up in the holiness around the throne of God every time we share in the liturgy. My worry is that we appear *not to expect it ever to happen*. We are not yearning for it. We have lost sight of it as the crown of our worshipping endeavour.[10]

Despite the enormous number of words written in, about and in response to *Common Worship*, a lack of confidence may still be discerned in the Church's liturgical endeavours. Some of this may be a reaction to the sheer volume of the *Common Worship* library, which, were we not living in a digital age, would need to be carried around in a wheelbarrow. Some of the lack of confidence may be more to do with the manifold pressures which act upon the parish priest and her lay colleagues in contemporary ministerial contexts where having enough time to focus on crafting and turning an act of liturgical worship may not be as high up the priority list as the priest and laity would have it be. At least some

---

9 Paul Gerhardt, 'The Duteous Day now Closeth', trans. Robert Bridges. *New English Hymnal* (Norwich: Canterbury Press, 1986), No. 253.

10 Perham, *New Handbook*, p. 5, emphasis mine.

of the anxiety is also perhaps a weakening of faith that the words and their associated gestures and actions do have the potential to transport us. We are losing confidence in the *lex orandi, lex credendi,* we are forgetting the preface to the Declaration of Assent, and the danger with that is that the liturgical encounter is reduced either to entertainment, to a functional duty or to something which aims primarily to make us feel good about ourselves for an hour or so. It ceases to be the space and time where we expect to be transformed.

What transport of delight

As we have discussed, exposure to liturgy can transport us, but it can also transform us. The joining together of words and movement with the space we are in can, indeed should, come together to effect some sort of change. Liturgy is sacramental and so, like a sacrament proper, effects a change.

Good definitions of liturgy will always refer to words, signs, symbols, silence, space, movement and so on. Liturgy is about far more than text on a page. It is, as has been discussed, about the way in which the ministerial and congregational texts inhabit their context. It is about the way in which the rubrics and notes point the minister towards possibilities for silence or movement, the use of symbol, the use of extempore or locally devised words, and the very centre of it is about the use of the deep texts of the tradition, the recourse to the words which the Church has spoken from the beginning, and the calling to mind that wherever we are and however we pray we are part of a family who does this work together. Good definitions of liturgy will also always recognize that liturgy itself is, in the best sense of the word, theatre. This is why taking care over the words, the movements, the gestures, the spaces and silences, the local and the universal, matters. These are the pseudo-sacramental manifestations of the reality that lies behind them. The liturgy matters because the liturgy points to the Kingdom, and like all sacramental pointers, they not only point to the inward and spiritual grace which they signify, but in their very act of pointing, manifestation happens. There are outward and visible signs here too, real signs, real pointers to a very real Kingdom. Every Sanctus points to the truth of the congregation of heaven. It points to that truth even when no one in the cold, empty church slogging through a miserable and uninspiring liturgy can perceive it. It points to it just as much as on the rare occasion when it seems as though angels really do descend around the altar and among the worshippers. The Sanctus points to the ministry of the angels because that ministry is always there, and so to seek to do liturgy well is not an exercise in arrogance or self-aggrandizement on the part of the priest and his people, nor is it a distraction from the 'real tasks of ministry', whatever we may believe those to be, because to seek to perform the liturgy well is to aspire to being a member of the community of heaven. To seek to pray together well is to want to be a family. Some of the liturgy is, of course, sacramental in the firmest sense of the definition, but all liturgy is sacramental in the broader sense, because all liturgy, whether a funeral, a marriage service, a family service on Good Friday, or the lighting of the first Advent candle of the season, points beyond itself to the mysterious Kingdom which lies just out of sight and yet close enough to touch.

I rather mourn the loss of the word 'transport' from the final verse of Fanny Crosby's hymn 'To God be the glory, great things he hath done'. Of course I understand the reason for the change, which is to do with the changing definition of the word transport, and the potential for those singing the hymn to have images of buses rather than heaven in their head. The word has been replaced in successive revisions of hymnals first by the word 'rapture', and then by the word 'worship', but the kinetic force of the original word is striking:

> But purer, and higher, and greater will be
> our wonder, our transport, when Jesus we see.[11]

---

11 Fanny Crosby, 'To God be the glory, great things he hath done' in *Brightest and Best: a choice collection of new songs, duets, choruses, invocation and benediction hymns for the Sunday school and meetings of prayer and praise*, ed. R. Lowry and W. H. Doane (New York: Biglow & Main, 1875).

Crosby's text offers the singer participation in the conviction that our present rejoicing is a reflection of, but nothing like as great as, that which we will experience when we come face to face with our Lord. The word transport has such motive energy that it reminds the worshipper that all liturgy, all worship and indeed the Christian life is infused with movement. Movement and being transported is an important theological theme.

Liturgical Theology in Context

Pastoral liturgy

Pastoral liturgy provides the possibility for transport. My ordaining bishop, in his Charge to my cohort of nervous deacons-to-be, reminded us that part of our calling is 'the telling of the Christian story attractively in a way that. . . reveals to people the God they hardly knew they were seeking'.[12] One of the glories of the parochial system of the Church of England is that these opportunities to discover with a group of people the God they hardly knew they were seeking are still manifold. The potential for chance encounters with the divine through the Church's liturgical ministry has never been higher. The resources which exist to aid the minister, lay or ordained, in the construction of thoughtful, confident, welcoming liturgy are remarkable both in their variety and quantity. Transforming the words on the page into a crucible for liturgical theology, as Fagerberg would have it be, is a wonderful and challenging calling.

I remain deeply grateful to my excellent training incumbent for teaching me very early on how to conduct a funeral in the absence of any mourners. Although the lesson was, in the moment, a practical one, it was also a profoundly theological one. He taught me at least three things on the day we went to the crematorium to conduct a funeral for a man for whom there was no one to

12 M. Perham, 'The Bishop of Gloucester's Ordination Charge 2005'. Unpublished manuscript.

mourn. The first thing was to read the story of the Rich Man and Lazarus,[13] because the leader of worship ought never to make assumptions about what has brought anyone to the place where they now are. That in itself was a crucial lesson to me as a young deacon. The second thing was about movement and touch. Even with no one in the congregation, the liturgical movements of the funeral, the reverencing of the coffin, the claiming of the liturgical space by methodical, deliberate and time-hallowed liturgical actions was just as valid, because of course there was a congregation there, made up of not only one living and one dead person, but of angels and archangels and all the heavenly host. The third thing he taught me in that brief but formative lesson was that you always use the entire liturgy. The words of the Church are the words of the Church, and everybody deserves them, or more correctly everyone is afforded equal access to them by the grace of God. And of course, my incumbent added, you never know if someone might be late for the funeral and arrive halfway through, and in doing so step into an environment which at least has the potential to transport them.

This movement, this transport, is perhaps what those worshippers at Evensong in the cathedral are reaching for description of when they talk about the service 'doing something to them'. Chance encounters with the liturgy have a high potential for transport because the worshipper comes with very little expectation of being transported. If there is expectation, it might of course be negative. We all have stories of being in the congregation at appalling acts of worship; we have all heard stories from friends and family of awful funerals where the vicar didn't even use the name by which the deceased was commonly known, or weddings where the officiating priest was so mind-numbingly dull, or the organist so incompetent, that the congregation were either paralysed with boredom or doubled up with laughter. In the small hours of the night those of us who are ordained or lay leaders of worship fret that somewhere out there someone is telling a story like that about a service we conducted.

---

13 Luke 16.19–31.

Sometimes the very purpose for going to church might seem to legislate against the attendee encountering the divine. The young man who goes to the crematorium in order to sit in the front row of a chapel devoid of personality to look at a wooden box containing the body of his mother for twenty minutes is probably entering into that act of worship with only one aim: that of enduring the experience with a degree of dignity. All liturgy, but pastoral liturgy in particular, must confidently assert that even in these most unlikely scenarios there are angels.

The cathedral

A few years ago I was invited to sum up the theological import of Salisbury Cathedral in a single word. The word I chose was 'up'. Salisbury Cathedral, in its architectural form, with its Gothic arches, largely clear windows, and slender spire pointing the way to heaven, and in its liturgy which is largely choral, and based on an unfussy pseudo-monastic modern catholic interpretation with very tall processional candles, long narrow processional banners, and lots of incense drifting into the roof space but very little use of the thurible, seeks to lift up the eyes and the hearts as well as the minds of worshippers.[14] There is movement, there is 'transport' going on even in static elements of the cathedral. I suppose I might sum up the principal liturgical theology of the cathedral as that of the Ascension. Other buildings and other contexts will find slightly differing dominant liturgical theologies. If asked to undertake the same exercise on the other cathedral which I know and love well, Gloucester, I instinctively ascribe to that house of prayer the word 'here', because my natural reaction to that building, with its *pulpitum* screen, wide nave and heavy warm Norman columns, is that of a place which speaks most naturally of the incarnation. Is the dominant theology of Gloucester Cathedral that of Christmas, I wonder? In a sense what I have just described is a rather artificial exercise and

---

14 T. Clammer (ed.), 'Salisbury Cathedral Draft Liturgical Plan' (Salisbury Cathedral Chapter, unpublished manuscript, 2016), p. 3.

of course any liturgical arena will be inspired by numerous seasonal and theological influences during the year. The discipline of identifying a single word to describe the dominant liturgical theology of a particular community and its building is, however, a useful, if inevitably subjective, one because it can help those who plan liturgical worship to identify in what way the regular or the occasional worshipper might be moved and transported by their encounter.

A multi-parish benefice

With the ever-increasing numbers of multi-parish benefices and with some clergy having a more 'episcopal' role, one of the challenges is, of course, maintaining some liturgical coherence across multiple liturgical arenas. Another is a relative lack of resources, at least compared to our previous example of a cathedral, both in terms of people and of easily accessible 'kit'. In my last post I remember filling my car with enormous quantities of stuff in the week before Easter and driving around my six churches depositing a portable font here, a Calvary cross there, and different sets of vestments and orders of service all over the place, not to mention enormous vacuum flasks of water for the renewal of baptismal vows in all my churches on Easter Day, all but one of which had no running water.

A number of challenges and opportunities present themselves when constructing liturgy for a large rural benefice where each church building might only be used once or twice a month and, during the great seasons of the year such as Christmastide or Holy Week and Easter, only for one service out of the whole period. Assuming that the entire round of Holy Week services will not be replicated in six locations – almost certainly the case in most rural benefices – how does it work to mark the Triduum? It may be that the only liturgy of the cycle to be celebrated in one church is that of Maundy Thursday, and the church in which the Good Friday liturgy will be held is not the one that was stripped the night before at the end of the liturgy of the Last Supper. Interestingly the majority of Church of England resources don't treat this issue in any depth,[15] and the popularly used Roman Catholic texts such as Elliot's *Ceremonies of the Liturgical Year* tend towards a liturgical purity which can be pastorally unhelpful. One example of this is the injunction that if there will not be a Good Friday liturgy in the church in which the Maundy Thursday Eucharist is celebrated, then the sacrament is returned to the tabernacle in the normal way at the end of the Mass. While there may be an internal coherence to this instruction, what it does is to deprive the congregation participating in that service of the extraordinary symbolism of the reservation elsewhere of the sacrament, and also, for any casual visitor or worshipper popping into the church on Good Friday, the powerful impact of the stripped sanctuary and the aumbry door standing open.[16] In the rural benefice in which I ministered we had to engage with this challenge, and ended up creating a tradition of beginning Good Friday with Morning Prayer in the Chapel of Repose of the church in which we had conducted the Maundy Thursday liturgy, and then walking the sacrament slowly to the church in which the Good Friday liturgy would take place. Over the few years that I was parish priest there this 'tradition' grew in popularity and resulted in a benefice walk on Good Friday leading up to the service in church. Obstacles such as the River Severn were overcome by commandeering a rowing boat from the local sailing club to row the worshippers and the Sacrament across the river! While a procession of the Blessed Sacrament is no part of the liturgical tradition of Good Friday, it seemed like an imaginative and engaging solution to a practical problem created by parochial reorganization and reduction in clergy numbers, had the result of offering a unifying experience to potentially disparate congregations, and was undertaken in such a manner that it was clear that what was happening

---

15 For example B. Gordon-Taylor and S. Jones, *Celebrating Christ's Victory: Ash Wednesday to Trinity* (London: SPCK, 2009), which is excellent, but makes the assumption that the Good Friday liturgy will be celebrated in the same liturgical space as that of Maundy Thursday.

16 P. Elliott, *Ceremonies of the Liturgical Year According to the Modern Roman Rite* (San Francisco: Ignatius Press, 2002), p. 104 para 206. Elliott discourages the celebration of the services of Holy Week in places with small congregations and few resources, preferring several congregations together in a larger building.

was solemn, and in no way the same as the chaotic and joyful Palm Sunday processions which had taken place in the various villages five days earlier. Those carrying the Sacrament, which was reserved in a simple ciborium and covered with a plain white veil, wore a very plain red stole, and there was no singing or chanting. There may be better or different ways to approach such challenges, and it would be good if the Church of England did more thinking in the public square about this. The solution thought up by my benefice is an example of liturgical theology in Fagerberg's model.

Conclusion

When I began teaching liturgy to ordinands and readers in training about eight years ago I used to divide my sessions into Principles and Practicalities. The principles were things about the liturgical and theological purpose, meaning and direction of the service, whereas practicalities were about where one sits or stands to take the service, and whether or not you provide a crèche. I have become less and less confident in the distinction, and I now believe that all of those practicalities are actually principles because they are to do with ordering the liturgical arena, welcoming the liturgical participants, and thus hallowing an environment where God, humanity and the world will meet, interact and create liturgical theology. Giving consideration to things like where a wedding couple will sit; whether or not this family need to be close to or far away from the coffin; whether people who arrive late, or in a wheelchair, or with children, have an honoured place in the assembly; whether there is enough assistance for people to navigate through the service without making the liturgy lumpy; whether there is consistency in movement and gesture so that the very beginnings of a pattern can be identified: these are the hallmarks of sound liturgical planning because what they aim to do is to hold and honour a space in which we create 'liturgy for whoever turns up',[17] so that whoever turns up might be transported.

---

17 To borrow a phrase from my one-time colleague Dr Sandra Miller.

Careful attention to the details – the choice of words, the amount of silence, where the seats will be, whether there will be movements, incense, what robes might be worn, how many of the words will be scripted and how many extempore – these things allow fellowship, they form 'the faithful'. More than that, they take seriously the fact that the Church, when she joins in liturgical worship, is actually doing liturgical theology, and that she believes that this worship is a sign, a foretaste and the sacrament of the life of the Kingdom which lies just beyond our senses, and in whose halls the rustle of angels' wings can just occasionally be heard.

I would like to return to that church service in about 1997 in which I first heard the collect for the lighting of the first candle of Advent. I don't suppose I could identify now and describe the precise nature of that act of worship and draw conclusions about the delicate blend of word, action, praise and prayer which the liturgical manuals suggest makes up a balanced act of worship. I think about that service often, however, because it was undoubtedly one of the moments when I was transported by the presence of God, and one of the moments where I think I have come closest to recognizing the Kingdom in our midst. I am grateful that those who prepared that act of worship had taken care over it. I am grateful that the elements of liturgy which the definitions so often refer to must have been there because I remember them. I am profoundly grateful for the collect itself, which has burned itself into my liturgical memory in a way that most of the other texts have not. I was not expecting to have an experience of transport when I went to church that morning, and I rather suspect that most moments which are truly transformational are unexpected also. The Lord Jesus described in that collect I committed to memory all those years ago, when I knew neither the prayer's origin, author nor provenance, emerges through the song, silence, words and movement of the liturgy so that suddenly or gradually, in quiet or in celebration, he is born in our hearts and, without us even noticing it, he is King of our lives.

7

On the Complexities of Defining the Unity of the Church: A Historical Reflection

CHARLOTTE METHUEN

Introduction and Personal Note

In autumn 2006, I unexpectedly received an invitation from Michael Perham to serve as the first Canon Theologian of the Cathedral and Diocese of Gloucester. He wanted, he told me, to appoint a woman to a senior post in the diocese, and none of the archdeacons or other senior staff were likely to step down in the near future. I accepted the invitation with pleasure, and, although geography meant that my contact with the diocese was sporadic (I was based initially in Oxford and subsequently in Glasgow), it proved, for me at least, an important step. Michael encouraged me to apply my historical knowledge and ecumenical interests to the current issues facing the Church of England, for the benefit of the diocese, and particularly the cathedral chapter and clergy. And so I gave an inaugural lecture on '"Each in our own native language": Reflections on Church, Catholicity and Culture',[1] addressed the cathedral chapter on 'The emerging shape of the Anglican communion 1867–2008', spoke to the diocesan pastoral conference on the question of 'The Pressure on the Church – Some ecclesiological reflections', and introduced the diocesan synod to the proposed Anglican Communion Covenant (an initiative which

---

1 This was published as '"From All Nations and Languages": Reflections on Church, Catholicity and Culture', in *The Anglican Covenant: Unity and Diversity in the Anglican Communion*, ed. Mark Chapman (London: Mowbray, 2008), pp. 123–42.

Michael strongly opposed, although out of respect for Archbishop Rowan, he abstained in the diocesan vote).

Michael's articulation of his vision for my session on 'The Pressure on the Church' illustrated his characteristic approach:

> If you could explain why the church is divided, why we can't agree about homosexuality, why there are arguments about the Covenant, and why some people are so disturbed by the idea of women in the episcopate, you would help a lot.

'No pressure on me, then', as I think I said at the beginning of my attempt to engage with this comprehensive task. But its articulation illustrated something that was of vital importance to Michael: division in the Church – whether the Church of England, the Anglican Communion, or the global Church – and how to live with it, were questions that he thought about a lot.

When in 2011 Michael became President of Affirming Catholicism, on whose board I had been serving since 2008, he offered insightful engagement with Affirming Catholicism's input into synodical processes, relating particularly, but not only, to the ordination of women. In January 2015, Michael sent a message of greeting to Affirming Catholicism's service to celebrate the passing of the legislation to allow women to become bishops in the Church of England, a service at which he had been due to preside:

> It has been for me an honour to be President of Affirming Catholicism and a more recent pleasure to have become a Vice President of WATCH. Both organizations have served in their different ways the kind of generous inclusive Catholicism in which I have long believed. I have delighted in the friendships made as we have worked together and seen one huge milestone reached in the vote in the General Synod last July. There is so much for which I have gratitude and so can identify fully with the thankfulness of today's celebration.

Michael took synods seriously, but he was also, as other essays in this volume illustrate, deeply aware of the need to ensure that members of synods are able to make informed decisions. He hoped, I think, that synodical engagement would help to fulfil his vision of 'generous inclusive catholicism' by giving space for differences to be articulated in ways that others could hear and understand, even if they did not agree.

This paper comes back to the questions which Michael invited me to address with his chapter and his clergy. It asks, not so much, why do divisions exist, but what, in the face of division, is the vision of unity that the Church is called to articulate and to live out? And it does this by exploring how the Church through its history has lived with difference.

The Myth of Early Christian Unity

One of the most profound insights offered by church historians over the past fifty years has been the recognition that, even in its earliest history, it is not possible to speak of a uniform, unified church. In his letter to the Ephesians, Paul calls Christians to recognize and live out their unity: 'I . . . beg you to lead a life worthy of the calling to which you have been called, with all humility and gentleness, with patience, bearing with one another in love, making every effort to maintain the unity of the Spirit in the bond of peace' (Eph. 4.1–3 [NRSV]) For, he affirms, 'There is one body and one Spirit, just as you were called to the one hope of your calling, one Lord, one faith, one baptism, one God and Father of all, who is above all and through all and in all' (Eph. 4.4–6). In the farewell discourses in John's Gospel, Jesus calls for Christians to be one: 'The glory that you have given me I have given them, so that they may be one, as we are one' (John 17.22). But even at this stage, the vision of these texts beloved by ecumenical theologians is being spoken into a situation in which Christians were not one. Rather, these texts are reminders that the followers of Christ belong together. And these biblical exhortations witness to the fact that from its beginning the Church has held together, more or less successfully, different and differing views.

Several examples of differences can be found in the New Testament. The question of the status of Gentile Christians divided

Paul and Peter in Acts, and the Council of Jerusalem took place in response (Acts 15). The Council made a decision: 'that we should not trouble those Gentiles who are turning to God, but we should write to them to abstain only from things polluted by idols and from fornication and from whatever has been strangled and from blood' (Acts 15.19–20 [NRSV]). On this question, the New Testament shows us a decision being made. But the New Testament also witnesses to other differences. Some of these were theological, relating to the status of Jesus Christ and his relationship to God, Christological questions which would come to dominate theological discussions from the second to the fifth century. Others related to expectations of the future: was the end of the world so close that it made no sense to plan for the future? Still others were structural: how was the Christian community to be organized? The Pauline epistles tend to conceive the ministries of the Church in terms of charisms, while the Pastoral epistles, probably a generation later, are more inclined to see ministry in terms of offices: deacon and bishop, perhaps female deacons and certainly widows. The New Testament witnesses to differences about the role of women, such as whether or not they can bear reliable witness or speak 'publicly' in church, while also affirming, in the words of Gal. 3.28: 'There is no longer Jew or Greek, there is no longer slave or free, there is no longer male and female; for all of you are one in Christ Jesus.' There are hints too in New Testament texts of disagreements regarding the benefits of marriage. In a context which expected the end of the world to occur imminently, was it worth marrying? Paul thought that it might well be better to remain celibate, although he recognized that passion might make marriage necessary for some (1 Corinthians 7.8–9).

Differences existed from the beginning, and it seems likely that Christian groups holding different views, structured in different ways, and with different Christian practices, existed alongside one another during the early centuries of the Church's history. Many of these differences were not easy to resolve. Even the question of the keeping of the Jewish Law, which is often assumed to have been settled with the Council of Jerusalem, or at the latest with the fall of Jerusalem in AD 70, in reality took far longer to settle than is often assumed. The *Didascalia Apostolorum* (*Teaching of the Apostles*), a church order probably dating to the early third century, witnesses to an ongoing discussion about the need for Christians to observe Jewish Law; churches are referred to as 'synagogues'; and the author is particularly interested in the question of whether women should take a ritual bath each month after menstruation or whether (as he argues) baptism is the single bath necessary for purification. The *Didascalia* offers evidence that the question at issue between Peter and Paul continued to be disputed for at least another 150 years.

The office of the bishops was emerging in this early period. Although some local churches may still have been overseen by presbyters (including in some cases women: *presbyterae*), by the third century bishops were becoming established and increasingly functioned as the definers of unity for their local church. Local here probably still meant single congregations, or in some cases perhaps the congregations in one city. The mid-third century saw the first record of synods, with a council called in Carthage by the city's bishop, Cyprian, to come to an agreement about what to do about the lapsed, that is, those who had denied their Christian faith under persecution, or betrayed it by sacrificing to the emperor or burning the Scriptures. What did the lapsed need to do in order to become reconciled to the Church and be received back into communion? Cyprian took the line that they could be reconciled (which displeased those of a stricter mindset), but held that oversight of this process was his responsibility as bishop, and not the responsibility of those who had held fast to their faith under persecution (which displeased these so-called confessors, especially since Cyprian had fled Carthage to avoid the persecution). This conflict led to a series of schisms, which focused on a disagreement about whether the lapsed could become clergy, and if they did, about the validity of the sacraments which these clergy administered. Cyprian was adamant that the sacraments of those who did not recognize his episcopal authority were not valid, so that those joining the 'catholic' church from these other groups should be rebaptized. Stephen, Bishop of Rome, disagreed, arguing that those baptized by schismatic or heretical groups need not be rebaptized. In 325, the Council of Nicaea took a position largely following Cyprian's: the lapsed could be readmitted to communion 'over a period of twelve years', but were not to be ordained; the clergy of the rigorist, Novatianist conviction (who taught that the lapsed were not to be readmitted to communion) were to have hands laid on them again; and followers of the heretical Paul of Samosata who wanted to join the Catholic Church were to be rebaptized. Cyprian's conviction that the doctrine of the Church defined its unity and the validity of its sacraments was upheld at Nicaea.

However, the Council did not settle the matter and controversy continued, leading to the establishment of the Donatist schism. In the early fifth century, Augustine would support Stephen's position, arguing that those baptized by the Donatists should not be rebaptized. Augustine held that the sacraments administered by the Donatists were valid but not yet effective; when Christians baptized by the Donatists joined the Catholic Church, their baptism became also effective. Augustine therefore did not advocate the rebaptism of anyone who had been baptized, using water, in the name of the Father and the Son and the Holy Spirit. Councils and consultation over practice elsewhere had helped to inform the decisions taken by Cyprian and Stephen, but after nearly two hundred years of conflict, it was Augustine, going against the Council of Nicaea, who formulated what would become the Western Church's policy on (re-)baptism. The Church lived for a long time in dispute on these questions, with schismatic, or even heretical, movements forming around the different positions, and probably a real difficulty sometimes in discerning what the differences really were.

Cyprian had wanted a united church, but it was in the fourth century, with the legalization of Christianity by the Emperor Constantine through the Edict of Milan (313), that the unity of the Church became not only a doctrinal question, but one which centred on the definition of doctrinal orthodoxy. Having chosen to legitimize Christianity, Constantine wanted a united church, which in his eyes meant a church which was agreed about doctrine and practice. The Council of Nicaea (325) was intended to bring this about, by legislating on the differences between the presbyter Arius and his bishop, Alexander of Alexandria. These differences centred on the question of Christ's divinity: was Christ divine in the same way as the Father, or not? Arius thought not, but the Council of

Nicaea agreed with Alexander. It resulted in the first draft of the Nicene Creed, and the exile of Arius, but here too this was not the end of the story. It would be over fifty years before the text that is now generally referred to as the 'Nicene Creed' (actually the Niceno-Constantinopolitan Creed) came into being, in 381 at the First Council of Constantinople, articulating a more developed form of the doctrine of the Trinity with great emphasis on the Holy Spirit. Christological debate continued. Fifty years later, in 431, the Council of Ephesus proclaimed the Virgin Mary to be *Theotokos* ('God-bearer') and in 451 the Council of Chalcedon articulated the relationship between the divine and human natures of Christ. By then, the Church had been struggling with Christological questions for nearly four hundred years.

The early Church, then, lived with difference. It engaged in long-term processes which sought agreement on questions of theology and practice. The Council of Nicaea pronounced on the correct calculation of the date of Easter, and on procedures for ordaining bishops as well as on the treatment of the lapsed and on Trinitarian doctrine. However, differences in practice probably continued in these areas, just as Christology continued to be debated. And many of the 'heretics' whose views were anathematized by Nicaea and subsequent councils did not change their views, but formed alternative Christian communities, some of which (such as the churches of the East) still exist today. The Ecumenical Councils from Nicaea to Chalcedon sought to define and impose unity within the Catholic Church, but in doing so, they also helped to bring about structural divisions and the separation of Christian communities which held different views.

The Complexities of Unity in the Medieval Church

The legalizing of Christianity in the Roman Empire brought a fundamental change in the being of the Church. From being a persecuted religious minority – albeit one with an increasingly high-profile membership – the Christian Church, and in particular its bishops, gained status in the Empire. In 380, the emperors

Theodosius I, Gratian and Valentinian II issued a decree, *Cunctos populos*, declaring Nicene Christianity to be the only religion of the Empire, and defining it as the only form of Christianity which was allowed to call itself Catholic. There was a tension between those Christians who believed the Christian Church to have sold out to imperial power and those who saw this development as a proper recognition of the status of Christianity and of the Christian God as constitutive of the Roman Empire. Augustine's *City of God* was written in the context of this debate after the sack of Rome by the Visigoths in 410, which left many Romans questioning the wisdom of abandoning traditional religion and the imperial cult. In the chaotic centuries which followed, the structures of the Christian Church, and particularly the emerging monastic orders, helped to preserve classical learning and were sometimes able to act as a stabilizing influence that came to be valued by ruling dynasties. Monastic-led missions, however, could easily function largely independently. Benedict composed his Rule in around AD 550, but it was not until Charlemagne declared in 789 that all monastic communities should live according to that Rule, and the development at around the same period of processes of papal authorization, that monastic orders became more clearly aligned to the Roman Church. The existence of competing narratives relating to the bringing of Christianity to (for instance) Ireland and Scotland witnesses to attempts to emphasize (or possibly assert) Rome's role in establishing these churches. Did the Church in Ireland originate from the efforts of Palladius, sent by Pope Caelestinus in 431, or from Patrick, born in Scotland, England or even Wales, and independent of any papal instruction? Was Christianity first taken to Scotland by Ninian, under the influence of Rome, or by Columba, coming independently from Ireland? These different narratives, which are of varying historical plausibility, witness to retrospective attempts to affirm the universality of Roman, papal authority and the unity of the Church that spread under its aegis.

The papacy, rather than synods or councils, is the key factor here. At around the time of the fall of Rome, the Bishop of Rome assumed the title *Pontifex Maximus*, which since the time of Constantine had been applied to the emperor, and which emphasized his role as mediator between earth and heaven. In the centuries to come, unity in the Western Church would increasingly be defined in terms of recognition of the pope's authority. In this way, the unity of the Western Church came to be centred on the papacy. The Bishop of Rome's claims to authority were a major factor in the schism between the Western and Eastern churches, which in 1054, ostensibly over the insertion of the *filioque* ('and the Son') clause into the description of the precession of the Holy Spirit in the Nicene Creed led to mutual excommunications by the Pope and the Patriarch of Constantinople. But attitudes towards papal authority defined responses to disagreement within the Western Church as well. The Waldensians, who emphasized poverty and sought to preach the gospel more directly to the people, ignoring the fact that Peter Waldo and his successors had been granted no official permission to preach, were rejected as heretical, while Franciscans, who emphasized poverty and sought to preach the gospel more directly to the people, but bound themselves to papal authority, became, alongside the Dominicans, a significant order of friars integrated into the Church.

But although authority rested ultimately with the pope, and orthodoxy and heresy – and with them the unity of the Church – were increasingly defined in terms of papal authority, medieval ecclesiastical structures were complex. Increasingly, the Church was structured according to several parallel hierarchies: diocesan structures in which clergy looked to bishops who in turn looked to archbishops and the pope; the Benedictine monastic orders in which individual monastic houses were integrated into provinces which looked to the pope; and, from the thirteenth century, the friars, also organized into houses, with their own separate provincial structures, also looking to the pope. Benedictines tended to be enclosed orders, which might play an important economic as well as spiritual role in a local region, but which tended not to stand directly in competition with parish clergy. Franciscans and Dominicans, by contrast, were called to preach – the official name of the Dominican order was the 'Order of Preachers' – and by the fourteenth and fifteenth centuries, friars were regularly being appointed to preach in parish churches alongside, or sometimes instead of, parish clergy. The resulting competition was considerable. Not only preaching rights were at stake: who could hear confessions, and who could preside at funerals? Parish clergy, defending their rights (and their incomes), claimed that the mendicant friars were not able to pronounce absolution since they did not properly speak on behalf of the bishop, and warned that those buried anywhere but in the parish churchyard would find themselves 'sons and daughters of damnation'.

A church defined by papal authority was deeply susceptible to alternative papal claims. When in 1378 Bartolomeo Prignano, Archbishop of Bari, was elected pope and took the name Urban VI, a group of cardinals soon reneged on their decision, electing Robert of Geneva as a rival pope later that year. Robert, who took the name Clement VII, established his papal court in Avignon. The Western Schism split the Church but also the European political landscape. For the next thirty years, the Roman pope was recognized by Denmark, England and Ireland, Flanders, the Holy Roman Empire, Hungary, Norway, Portugal, Poland, Sweden, the Republic of Venice, and other City States of northern Italy, while the Avignon pope was supported by France, Aragon, Castile and León, Cyprus, Burgundy, Savoy, Naples, Scotland and Owain Glyndwr's rebellion in Wales. The situation became even more complex when a third pope, Alexander V, was elected by the Council of Pisa in 1409, to be succeeded in 1410 by John XXIII. The situation of competing popes was resolved at the Council of Constance, convened by John XXIII, and recognized by Gregory XII, by then pope in Rome, which asserted the authority of a Council of the Church's bishops over the pope and elected Martin V in 1417. Martin V was finally recognized by the Avignon papacy in 1429. This crisis in papal authority gave strength to conciliarism, the idea that councils of bishops had the supreme authority over the pope.

All this should not be taken to imply that theology could not be a challenge to orthodoxy or unity. Medieval theologians could be, and were, investigated and excommunicated for heresy. The Western Church had a fundamental doctrinal and liturgical unity, but it also lived with difference, legislating, for instance, to allow communion of both kinds among the Utraquists in Bohemia in the wake of John Huss's execution at the Council of Constance. Regional practice was probably better regulated and more consistent than transregional practices, and regional synods of bishops and convocations of clergy played a part in promulgating common practices among diocesan clergy. Quite how the monastic houses and mendicant orders fitted into these often remained unclear, and an increasing point of contention. Moreover, while the relative authorities of pope and emperor had long been disputed, by the end of the fifteenth century conflict was deepening around questions of the relationship between the Church and local territorial rulers, particular in the German lands.

The Reformation and the Localization of Unity

The unity of the medieval Church was, then, not uncomplicated. In the German lands, there is much evidence for the complexity and ambiguity of the Church's situation. The Duke of Jülich-Berg, for instance, whose lands technically fell under the jurisdiction of the Archbishop of Cologne, rejected the archbishop as a 'foreign power'; in the fifteenth century, a 'Territorial Dean' (*Landesdechant*) was appointed who was made responsible for the ecclesiastical, and thus for the spiritual, affairs of the territory. Similarly, in Wittenberg the Electors of Saxony had negotiated papal privileges for the All Saints Foundation (the *Allerheiligenstift*) that they had established at their Castle Church in Wittenberg, which consequently stood directly under the pope's authority and was not answerable to the Bishop of Brandenburg, and these privileges were also extended to Wittenberg's parish church. In consequence the Bishop of Brandenburg's authority in Wittenberg was severely curtailed by the first decade of the sixteenth century. The bishop several times sought to place Wittenberg under an interdict – that is, a ban on the celebration of the Mass and other liturgical rites there – but in practice the interdict had little effect on Wittenberg's liturgical life, and in 1513 the town council claimed that the bishop had no authority over either the town or the archdeaconry in which it lay. By the early sixteenth century, rulers of German territories and city states were already seeking to assert their spiritual authority in local territories. The step towards the definition of territorial, local, churches was a smaller one than might initially seem the case if a unified 'Western Christendom' is assumed.

Within the German territories, the Reformation gave rise to a range of different understandings of the unity of the Church. The magisterial and princely Reformations tended to assume that all the people of one territory would have one confession, and the 1555 Peace of Augsburg was based on this principle: *cuius regio, eius religio* – 'the religion of the ruler is the religion of the people'. This represented a re-expression of the fundamental principle of Christendom, the assumption that the Church should encompass all people in one place or territory. Calvin emphasized that the visible Church would be a *corpus permixtum*, a 'mixed body' made up of both those who were elect and those who were not, in contrast to the attempts by some more radical reformers to restrict membership of their churches to those who could be certain of their election.

In German contexts, the focus on the territorial identity of the local church tended to be accompanied, as had been the case for the Church under Constantine, by a doctrinal statement defining the faith to be held and taught in the particular territorial church and the way that that church was to function. The Church Order drafted for the Duchy of Württemberg in 1559 thus included not only a confession of faith, but instructions relating to the form and frequency of divine service, instructions for the organization of schools and the university, the poor chest, the ordering of marriage, the regulation of physicians and magicians, visitations and town clerks. The intention was to define a church which, while it included everyone, would be consistent in faith and practice throughout Württemberg. The distinctions between how that consistency in faith and practice was articulated – and thus how churches looked – in different local contexts gave rise to differences which came to be identified as confessional markers: Protestants used vernacular Scriptures and liturgy, while Catholics worshipped in Latin; Protestants received communion in both kinds (bread and wine) and allowed their clergy to marry, while Catholics did not. But Protestants did not agree among themselves, and these differences divided them into different groups of churches which became identified as confessions: Lutherans tended to be more open to the retention of images in their churches; they used the Apocrypha in their worship; their worship often (although by no means always) continued to be quite liturgical; they made use of hymns to help teach the faith. In contrast the churches of the Reformed tended to be more austere; the focus of worship was on extempore prayer; if congregational singing took place in worship, it took the form of metrical psalms. Some Reformed churches not only rejected pilgrimages and processions but abandoned the calendar altogether, ceasing to celebrate Christmas and even Easter.

The definition of the Church as 'the community of the faith in which the Word of God was truly preached and the sacrament properly celebrated' was common to many parts of the Reformation, appearing in (among others) the Augsburg Confession, Calvin's Institutes and England's Thirty-Nine Articles. Here the Church is seen not in terms of its hierarchy and obedience to that hierarchy, but in terms of agreement about what constitutes the true preaching of the Word and proper administration of the sacraments. In the German and Swiss lands, in consequence, the Reformation gave rise to a new emphasis on theological conformity. These differences centred on the understanding of Christ's presence in the Eucharist, although there was also considerable disagreement about what aspects of the Church's teachings were essential to salvation. The interpretation of particular passages of Scripture, such as Matthew 26.26 ('This is my body') became fundamental to the definition of confessional identity. Increasingly, therefore, within confessionally focused Protestant churches hermeneutics and ecclesiology were closely intertwined. Luther, Zwingli and Calvin all believed that the authority to interpret Scripture lay with individual believers inspired by the Holy Spirit, and should not be claimed by the papacy and the curia. However, this begged the question of how different interpretations were to be reconciled. In the late sixteenth century, Lutherans developed a *regula fidei*, or 'rule of faith', in the shape of the Formula of Concord and the Book of Concord, which were intended to determine the correct interpretation of disputed passages of Scripture and to unite Luther's followers in different regions. Reformed churches appealed to their own catechisms and confessions of faith: the Geneva and the Heidelberg Catechisms, the *Consensus Tigurinus* or 'Zürich Agreement', the Belgic and Scots Confessions. Visitations continued to show, however, that many people in parishes had little understanding of the faith they were meant to confess. And, importantly, where confessions existed alongside each other, people lived together across those differences. Lutherans served, for instance, in the Catholic cathedral chapter of Bamberg, although they could not become bishop, or joined in with the Minster's Corpus Christi procession in Essen, although they no longer believed in a lasting presence of Christ in the host. Confessional differences did not preclude the kind of communication which went far beyond more-or-less tolerant coexistence.

Moreover, the status of confessional statements varied from church to church. In England, the Forty-Two Articles of 1553 became the Thirty-Nine Articles of 1571 which, in terms of their theology, took a generally Reformed line. However, whether clergy, teachers and magistrates were expected to subscribe to the Thirty-Nine Articles remained somewhat unclear; from 1604, clergy were expected to confirm that they were 'agreeable to the Word of God'. The example of the Church of England also shows how the use of different wording in different contexts could lead to theological ambiguity. Thus, the Thirty-Nine Articles affirmed that in the Lord's Supper, 'The Body of Christ is given, taken, and eaten, in the Supper, only after an heavenly and spiritual manner. And the means whereby the Body of Christ is received and eaten in the Supper, is Faith' (article 28). This interpretation reflected that found in the third exhortation of the 1559 Book of Common Prayer (which appeared as the second exhortation in Cranmer's 1548 order for the Lord's Supper and the 1549 BCP), which explained that in the Lord's Supper 'we spiritually eat the flesh of Christ, and drink his blood, then we dwell in Christ and Christ in us, we be one with Christ, and Christ with us'. It is presumably in the context of this exhortation that we should understand the combination, in the 1559 Prayer Book, of the words from the 1549 BCP and the 1552 BCP to be used in the distribution of communion: 'The body of our lord Jesu Christ, which was given for thee, preserve thy body and soul into everlasting life [1549]: take and eat this in remembrance that Christ died for thee, feed on him in thine heart by faith, with thanksgiving [1552].' However, it is clear that some of those who received the bread and wine at the hands of English priests took the 1549 formulation to imply that Christ was really and physically present in the eucharistic elements.

In the English Church, which was seeking to hold together the faith (and the faithful) of a nation, the approach taken to unity tended to be that of orthopraxis – with more emphasis laid on conformity of practice, shown largely by attendance at Sunday service – rather than that of orthodoxy – a shared confession of faith. In contrast, the approach taken north of the border, in neighbouring Scotland, was more akin to that of Geneva, with a strong emphasis on church discipline and a more theologically rigorously defined praxis. Such rigour looked attractive to English theologians who had experienced the Church in Geneva or Frankfurt-am-Main as exiles under Mary I, but this greater focus on rigour was not attractive to Elizabeth I, and although it was highly influential in Oliver Cromwell's interregnum, it lost ground in England at the Restoration. Nonetheless, the English Church going forward into the seventeenth century was the inheritor of different ecclesiologies and, with them, of different understandings of what defined unity: a conviction that the Church should, and must, include all the people of England, an understanding that shared faith was defined by shared practice, and a view that shared faith was rooted in an agreed confessional statement, rooted in a particular reading of Scripture. Preserving the balance between these three aspects was a challenge which faced all magisterial churches of the Reformation, but going forward the Church of England was unusual (and perhaps in Western Europe unique) in using the Book of Common Prayer, rather than a church order or confession of faith, as the primary marker of its unity.

Unity and the Anglican Communion

When, in the context of nineteenth-century mission and colonial expansion, the Anglican Communion began a process of conscious self-definition, it was initially to the Prayer Book that it turned. In 1878, at the second Lambeth Conference, the assembled bishops asserted that 'communion in worship is the link which most firmly binds together bodies of Christian men'. Affirming 'that the Book of Common Prayer, retained as it is, with some modifications, by all our Churches, has been one principal bond of union among them', they suggested that 'such communion in worship may be endangered by excessive diversities of ritual' (Recommendation 7). Similarly, recognizing the importance of the Book of Common Prayer as 'not the possession of one diocese or province, but of all', in 1888 the Lambeth Conference recommended 'that no particular portion of the Church should undertake revision without seriously considering the possible effect of such action on other branches of the Church" (Resolution 10). This concern for the Book of Common Prayer as the foundation of unity led to some caution in commending its revision. In 1948, the Lambeth Conference reiterated that 'the Book of Common Prayer has been, and is, so strong a bond of unity throughout the whole Anglican Communion', arguing that 'great care must be taken to ensure that revisions of the Book shall be in accordance with the doctrine and accepted liturgical worship of the Anglican Communion' (Resolution 78.a). In 1958, the Lambeth Conference reiterated the importance of 'features in these books which are effective in maintaining the traditional doctrinal emphasis and ecclesiastical culture of Anglicanism and therefore should be preserved' (Resolution 74.b), but did not attempt to define these more closely. Nonetheless, the Lambeth Conferences have long affirmed the liturgical aspects of Anglican identity and unity.

At the same time, there has been a growing recognition that the foundations of Anglican unity may need more explicit definition. Successive Lambeth Conferences had discussed the basis of unity, and the 1888 Conference had approved the Chicago-Lambeth quadrilateral as 'a basis on which approach may be by God's blessing made towards home reunion'. However, the quadrilateral soon became understood as summarizing the foundation of Anglican being:

a. The Holy Scriptures of the Old and New Testaments, as 'containing all things necessary to salvation', and as being the rule and ultimate standard of faith.

b. The Apostles' Creed, as the baptismal symbol; and the Nicene Creed, as the sufficient statement of the Christian faith.

c. The two sacraments ordained by Christ himself – Baptism and the Supper of the Lord – ministered with unfailing use of Christ's words of institution, and of the elements ordained by him.

d. The historic episcopate, locally adapted in the methods of its administration to the varying needs of the nations and peoples called of God into the unity of his Church. (Resolution 11)

The 1930 Lambeth Conference affirmed that the Anglican Communion was made up of 'duly constituted dioceses, provinces or regional Churches in communion with the See of Canterbury . . . bound together not by a central legislative and executive authority, but by mutual loyalty sustained through the common counsel of the bishops in conference' (Resolution 49.c). This vision was supported until the mid-twentieth century by personal contacts arising from the reality that the vast majority of the bishops of the Anglican Communion had been trained in either England or the USA. As the churches and provinces of the Anglican Communion became more locally rooted, there was a need for a 'renewed sense of responsibility for each other', expressed through 'partnerships of prayer', sacrificial and effective sharing of resources, whether human or financial, and 'a readiness to learn from each other' (Lambeth 1968, Resolution 67). The establishment of the Anglican Consultative Council by the 1968 Lambeth Conference was an attempt to support not only bishops, but also clergy and laity from across the Communion in deepening their contacts with one another. Similarly, in 1978 the then Archbishop of Canterbury, Donald Coggan, called the first Primates' Meeting 'as an opportunity for "leisurely thought, prayer and deep consultation"'. Both these initiatives manifested a growing recognition that unity is rooted in relationships, and that relationships take time. Across the Anglican Communion, it is not only the 'synodical' structures of the Lambeth Conference, Anglican Consultative Council and Primates' Meeting, but also places of encounter such as diocesan partnerships and the Anglican Communion's networks that enable communication and deepen unity.

Conclusion

It is apparent from this survey of understandings of unity across Christian history that disagreement has characterized the Church since its beginnings. It is also clear that 'generous inclusive catholicism' has not been a key way in which the Church has thought about what its unity entailed. It is, in the end, relatively easy to explain why the Church is divided. To start with, we read the Bible differently, and this leads us (for example) to different understandings of how human beings are gendered, and what that gender means for the exercise of authority or the forming of relationships, as well as to different understandings of Christ, or of the Eucharist. We have different understandings of what constitutes the Church, whether doctrine or church order are key, whether we are seeking to hold people together or sift people out, and so we disagree about the proper vision for the local congregation, let alone about the shape of the Anglican Communion. It is relatively easy to see why we differ. Christians have always differed. What is much harder is to see how to respond to those differences. Christian history, as this chapter has shown, abounds with models of unity formed through exclusion. Although in reality differences were never as clear-cut as theological pronouncements would suggest, the Church of England's decision to live with difference and hold together apparently mutually exclusive beliefs and practices is without clear precedent. If this vision – which Michael Perham undoubtedly shared – is to become a lived reality, the Church of England will need a strong commitment to education and communication, and to the facilitation of processes which will build trust and overcome the divisions within the Church, on questions of churchmanship as well as the ordination of women and sexuality. The additional challenge that now faces the Church of England is to demonstrate how its continued commitment to the validity of positions that much of society has come to view as deeply discriminatory can be lived out in ways that are recognizably neither sexist nor homophobic.

8

The Journey that Changed Us[1]

PAULA GOODER

Reflections on the way in which the journey towards the consecration of women to the episcopate has shaped the life and ecclesiology of the Church of England.

A personal note: I was deeply involved in the process that led up to the passing of the legislation in 2014 which made provision for the consecration of women as bishops, serving on committees that drew up initial drafts of legislation and then more latterly on the steering committee for the legislation (both that which failed in 2012 and that which passed in 2014). Throughout, the journey towards the final passing of that legislation was supported and helped by key people not on those committees. There was no one more influential in this than Michael Perham, whose unfailing dedication played a large part in ensuring its eventual success. On this issue Michael combined an unfailing vision for what should be with a deep pragmatism for what could be achieved. In this and in many other areas I am indebted to him.

Journeys change us. The act of setting out; the decisions we make as we go; the people and events we encounter along the way all ensure that we end our journey a different person from the one who set out. As Heraclitus is reported to have said, 'You cannot

---

1 Parts of this chapter appeared in a different form as an essay in *Vashti's Banquet: Voices from Her Feast: Essays to Mark the 25th Anniversary of the Ordination of the First Woman Diocesan Bishop in the Anglican Communion: The Rt Rev'd Penelope Ann Bansall Jamieson*, ed. Jenny Chalmers and Erice Fairbrother (Auckland: Council for Anglican Women's Studies, 2015). I am very grateful to the editors of that volume for giving me the permission to reproduce parts of that essay here.

step into the same river twice, for other waters are continually flowing on': both the river and the person stepping into it change, so the same action will never be exactly the same as the time before.

In the same way the Church of England's journey towards consecrating women as bishops has changed it. We are a different church now from that which we were when we began the journey. On one level this is a blindingly obvious thing to say – the Church of England now has both female and male bishops – but on another it is a more subtle point with a greater level of significance. It is not just the end of the journey (the consecration of female bishops) that has changed the Church but the very journey itself. The journey – and the way it was undertaken – has shaped and changed the Church of England and it is upon this journey that I would like to reflect in what follows.

Women and (Ordained) Ministry in the Church of England[2]

The year 1975 is often cited as the year which marked the beginning of the journey towards ordaining women as bishops. That was the year in which the General Synod passed a motion that declared that there are 'no fundamental objections to the ordination of women to the priesthood'. In some ways 1975 was the start of something new – a movement towards legislation in the General Synod – but in other ways it simply marked another step along the journey that had begun many years before.

Sean Gill argues that the origins of the movement towards the ordination of woman can be found in the revival of religious communities in the mid-nineteenth century, since these communities gave women a context within which they could follow their sense of religious vocation that called them into service of God and

---

2 A very good outline of this history can be found in *Women Bishops in the Church of England? A Report of the House of Bishops' Working Party on Women in the Episcopate* (London: Church House Publishing, 2004), often otherwise known as the Rochester Report.

the Church.[3] This revival was significant since it acknowledged that a woman's vocation could be to something other than marriage and a family. By the beginning of the twentieth century there were several hundred women in full-time ministry in the Church of England, thanks to the formation of the order of deaconesses by Elizabeth Ferard in 1861,[4] and the foundation of the Church Army by Wilson Carlile, which began training women as Church Army sisters in 1889.[5]

This nineteenth-century shift in attitude that allowed for the possibility that women might feel a vocation to serve the Church in more recognized roles paved the way in the early twentieth century for arguments in favour of the ordination of women. Leading campaigners such as Maude Royden – who was a preacher and a suffragist – argued strongly for women to be admitted to Holy Orders. The response from the Lambeth Conferences of 1920 and 1930 was that the order of deaconesses was indeed an order of ministry, but it was the only order that was or could be open to women.[6]

This attitude remained largely in place for the next forty-five years. The exception to it was the admission in 1969 of women as lay readers: nationally authorized lay ministers who are permitted to preach, lead worship and offer pastoral care. On one level the date of the admittance of women to this nationally recognized lay ministry is shockingly late. There are only two nationally licensed and recognized lay ministries within the Church of England – lay readers and evangelists. Women had been able to be admitted as

---

3 See Sean Gill, *Women and the Church of England: From Eighteenth Century to Present* (London: SPCK, 1994), p. 163.

4 For more on the development of the order of deaconesses, see Henrietta Blackmore (ed.), *The Beginning of Women's Ministry: The Revival of the Deaconess in the Nineteenth-Century Church of England*, first edition (Woodbridge, UK; Rochester NY: Boydell Press, 2007).

5 For more on Marie Carlile who ran the women's training college within the Church Army, see http://www.mariecarlile.co.uk/Contents%202.htm (accessed 18/05/2015).

6 'The order of deaconesses is for women the one and only order of the ministry which has the stamp of apostolic approval, and is for women the only order of the ministry which we can recommend . . .' See *Rochester Report*, p. 120.

evangelists since 1889; it took another eighty years for them to be admitted to be lay readers. On the other hand it is important to note that, late though it be, the move to admit women to reader ministry indicated a fundamental shift in attitudes to women's preaching and licensed ministry, a shift that set in train the movement towards opening all three orders of ordained ministry to women.

Although it took nearly one hundred years, the incipient change of attitude that was signalled in 1975 must find its roots in the thousands of women who followed their call by God into ministry within the Church, whether it was with religious communities or as deaconesses, Church Army sisters or, more latterly, as lay readers. The ministry of these many women as well as the campaigning work of people like Maude Royden began to shift attitudes to women's ministry more broadly, and then to women's ordained ministry more specifically.

It is worth taking the time, however, to reflect on one of the unintended consequences of this shift. This is that discussions about 'women's ministry' very quickly became discussions solely about the ministry of ordained women. This was inevitable and right. The Church was, in my view, diminished by not allowing women to seek ordination. Nevertheless, the nature of the discussion has become such that the phrase 'women's ministry' has become synonymous with ordained ministry, so that the ministry of the order of deaconesses, of Church Army sisters, of female lay readers, as well as the ministry of countless millions of women with no official recognition from church structures, can, at times, be felt to be lacklustre and less than ideal.

We should be clear that it was not just discussions about the ordination of women that focused attention onto ordained ministry; nor has this focus affected only women. Nevertheless, it is worth noting that the emphasis on discussion about women's ministry being the ministry of *ordained* women has contributed to the general lack of widespread conversation about the ministry of non-ordained people – both men and women. Now that women are present in all three orders of ordained ministry within the Church of England, it is more than time to do some remedial work on our attitudes to ministry more broadly.[7] In particular there is a great need to find ways to recognize and celebrate those servants of Christ whose ministry, either in their daily work and lives or within the Church, bring about God's Kingdom on earth. Our discussion about ministry should not stop but, at long last, we now have the opportunity to change its primary focus.

Deacons, priests and bishops

If the sweep of history from the late nineteenth century to the late twentieth century provides a very general backdrop to the ordination of women, as we have already noted, the period from 1975 onwards provides the specific context within which the discussion about women's ordination took place. Following the 1975 General Synod motion that declared that there were are 'no fundamental objections to the ordination of women to the priesthood', a second motion in 1978 that asked for legislation to remove barriers to the ordination of women to the priesthood and their consecration to the episcopate (in other words the motion that asked for the principle to be turned into practice) failed in the House of Clergy. Six years later, in 1984, a motion that requested legislation to permit the ordination of women to the priesthood did pass and, while that legislation was being drawn up, another motion was passed that permitted women to be ordained as deacons.

These two motions (1984 and 1986) on one level marked a significant development but on another level committed the Church of England to a particular form of development which some provinces around the Anglican Communion adopted and others did not. In others words, by passing these motions the General Synod of the Church of England split the threefold order of ministries apart so that women could be ordained first just to the diaconate (1986), then to the diaconate and the priesthood (1992) and only

---

7 It is great to observe that this work is beginning to be done and is represented in the recent report GS2056, *Setting God's People Free*. It is a good start but there is much still to be done in this area.

finally to all three orders of ministry (2014). I would argue that this decision exacerbated a tendency to divide 'orders of ministry' one from another: a tendency which has had a great impact upon the way in which the Church of England now thinks about ministry in general.

I noted above the unintended but increased clericalism that emerged from the need to focus attention on the importance of introducing the ministry of ordained women into the Church of England. The division of the threefold order of ministry is another unintended consequence of the *way* in which the debate about women's ordination has been enacted. The Church of England has always had a tendency to over-emphasize the differences between each order of ministry but the decision to ordain women in stages appears to have exacerbated this tendency.

The problem manifests itself in an over-focused attention on the so-called uniqueness of each order. This is something that is easier to do with episcopacy, harder with priesthood and almost impossible to do with the diaconate. In other words the nature of a particular order of ministry is described largely in terms of what makes that order unique. As a result, episcopacy is described in terms of the role of oversight and the function of providing a focus of unity and priesthood in relation to the sacraments.

Two particular issues emerge from this. The first is that there is little about the diaconate that makes it unique: bishops and priests continue to be deacons and there is nothing that a deacon does that a bishop or priest cannot do. As a result the diaconate is an under-defined and under-celebrated order of ministry. The second issue is that episcopal character is far more than 'just' effective oversight and being a focus of unity; just as priestly character is far more than 'just' effective sacramental ministry. I know of no priests who wish their ministry to be solely sacramental – indeed sacramental ministry only finds its meaning and focus through pastoral care, the preaching of the word and incarnational presence at the heart of a community, roles which could easily be cast as 'diaconal'.

The reality is that the threefold order of ministry – bishop, priest and deacon – should be held together, and celebrated together. Seeking the uniqueness of an order of ministry skews its focus in an unhelpful way. There are points of uniqueness but these only get their proper shaping when held together with the other two orders (in fact they only get their true shaping when held together with the ministerial life of the whole Church, lay and ordained). The way in which the Church of England made its decisions about the ordination of women has intensified the tendency to define bishops, priests and deacons in isolation from each other and as a result has had a great impact on its overall definition of ordained ministry.

A Brief Additional Note on the Permanent Diaconate

At first when women were ordained as deacons but not as priests or bishops, it was often observed that new life had been breathed into the permanent diaconate. The same could also be said in a different way of the deaconess movement founded by Elizabeth Ferard in 1861, but it could not be said today. Although there are a good number of permanent deacons who feel called to that ministry, they often report a level of institutional dis-ease with the role – and sometimes even confusion about what a permanent deacon is called to be and do.

The reality of the current situation in the Church of England is that in most people's minds we do not so much have a threefold order of ministry as a two-and-a-half-fold order, with the half being a transitional deacon's year before priesting. There is much creative thinking, however, that can be done around a permanent diaconate. This is especially so when that thinking is influenced by the concept of a deacon as commissioned agent or go-between which, as with conversation around the ministry of the whole Church, can be reinvigorated now that we no longer need to talk about women's ordained ministry as much as was necessary in the latter quarter of the twentieth and first decade and a half of the twenty-first centuries.[8]

---

8 For more on a renewed understanding of the diaconate in the light of a recalibrated view of the Greek word *diakonos*, see P. Gooder, 'Diakonia in the New Testament: A Dialogue with John N. Collins', *Ecclesiology* 3.1 (2006), pp. 33–56.

My own view is that a careful exploration of the New Testament evidence reveals that there is a much greater overlap between 'missioners' and 'deacons' than is normally acknowledged and that there is creative room for exploring this strand as one element of a permanent diaconate that could strengthen and animate the life of the Church in the twenty-first century.

Unity and Diversity

Thus far in this chapter I have reflected two unintended but powerful impacts of the discussions about the ordination of women on the life and ecclesiology of the Church of England today. They may come across as 'negative' impacts, but I would not class them as such. They are simply consequences of the way in which the debates unfolded but they do not need to stay that way. Identifying them and seeking to address them will, in their own way, shape and change the life of the Church in the future. A third impact of the debate about the ordination of the women first to the priesthood and then to the episcopate had unintended consequences on the life and ecclesiology of the Church of England and is the most controversial of the points to be explored here.

Both in 1992, after the passing of the legislation that allowed women to be ordained as priests, and in 2014 along with the legislation for the consecration of women as bishops, the House of Bishops made provision for those who could not in conscience accept the ordained ministry of women.

The Act of Synod

Following the vote in November 1992, in January 1993 the House of Bishops committed itself to 'accommodating a diversity of convictions, particularly in matters relating to the Church's sacramental life'.[9] What this meant in practice was the Episcopal Ministry

---

9 House of Bishops, *The Manchester Statement* (1993), p. 5.

Act of Synod (the Act of Synod). This sat alongside provisions already in place in the 1992 measure, which allowed parishes to pass resolutions that declared that they would not accept a woman priest celebrating Holy Communion or pronouncing absolution (Resolution A) or that they would not accept a woman as their incumbent (Resolution B). The Act of Synod added to these a third resolution (Resolution C) which allowed parishes to request alternative episcopal oversight from a Provincial Episcopal Visitor or PEV (these quickly became known as flying bishops).

Opinion on the wisdom of this House of Bishops decision is, to put it mildly, varied. Those parishes that passed Resolution C view the Act of Synod as the mechanism which made space for them to remain within the Church of England. On the other hand many supporters of the ordination of women regard it as the mechanism which fostered division within the church structures and encouraged an ongoing attitude of hostility towards the ministry not only of ordained women but also of men ordained alongside them.

There can be no doubt that the Act of Synod ensured a continued breadth of tradition within the Church of England – something that has been an important part of our self-definition from the Elizabethan Settlement onwards – but a number of questions remain. One is the question of the nature of the unity that the Act of Synod enabled and whether in keeping people within the Church it ended up dividing them from each other. The lived expression of the Act of Synod differed from diocese to diocese; in some dioceses the provisions of the Act did allow people with different viewpoints to live together to some extent, but in other dioceses the provisions seemed to build a high and impenetrable wall between different groups.

Another question arising from the Act of Synod focuses on the cost of the decision and whether that cost was shared equally throughout the Church. It is certainly the case that many ordained women felt that they were asked to bear the brunt of the cost of that decision in a way that was often not experienced by the bishops who enacted it. Yet another question is whether the establishment of Provincial Episcopal Visitors provided an implicit ecclesiological permission for episcopal territorial incursions (i.e. bishops from one province being sent into other provinces without the permission of that province). This is an issue that continues to rumble around the whole Anglican Communion, though it is entirely possible that such incursions would have taken place anyway, even without the implicit permission of the establishment of Provincial Episcopal Visitors.

There are of course many answers to these questions from different voices within the Church, with some seeing the Act of Synod in a much more positive light than others. It is not necessary here to adjudicate finally on these questions, not least because we are still living out the response to some of the questions, but it is important to recognize that the 1993 Act of Synod provided a vital context to the decisions that were later made about women's ordination to the episcopacy. In 1993 the House of Bishops made an ecclesiological decision about the nature of the Church of England – a decision that can be summed up as the attempt to ensure that a wide breadth of views about the ordination of women could be held together within its structures. The House of Bishops' 2014 guidelines that accompanied the legislation continued to reflect this decision, albeit in a slightly different form.

The Five Guiding Principles

The 2014 measure was as simple as it is possible to be. Four clauses long, it made lawful the consecration of women as bishops and established a few other principles (including, slightly uncomfortably, an exemption of this legislation from the equalities act).[10] This legislation was much simpler than the legislation that was proposed in November 2012 but that failed to get the necessary two-thirds majority in all three houses of General Synod. What made it acceptable to the General Synod as a whole were the additional provisions placed around it by the House of Bishops. These included both a declaration that laid out provisions for those who feel unable to receive the ministry of women bishops or priests

---

10 The contents of the measure can be found in GS 1925B.

and the Five Guiding Principles. It is highly unlikely that, without this additional material from the House of Bishops, the legislation would have passed.

The Five Guiding Principles reflect the conviction that clarity provides more confidence than vagueness. As a result, they are unequivocal about the decision that has been made to ordain women to all three orders of ordained ministry and the need for those within the Church of England to accept that this decision has been made. At the same time they seek to promote a space fully within the Church of England, within which those who are unable to receive the ministry of the Church of England can flourish.

The key feature of the Guiding Principles is that they *must* all be kept together. Provision is made for those who feel unable to receive the ministry of women bishops or priests on the clear understanding that they accept that 'those whom it [the Church of England] has duly ordained and appointed to office are true and lawful holders of the office which they occupy and thus deserve due respect and canonical obedience' [clause 1] and [clause 2] that the Church of England has made a clear decision on this matter. This is important. Until 2014 I heard it said on more than one occasion that the Church of England was a church that both did and did not ordain women. The five guiding principles are different from the provisions in the Act of Synod in that they are unequivocal about the decision that has been made. The Church of England is a church in which women are ordained as priests and consecrated as bishops. Nevertheless provision has been made – gladly and wholeheartedly – for those who hold a different view.

There can be no doubt that the legislation that was passed in 2014 was integrally shaped by the journey that brought us to that point. The many discussions about the nature of episcopacy; the experience of living with the consequences of the Act of Synod; the different options (such as the establishment of a Third Province or the automatic transfer of episcopal authority to another bishop) that were explored and discarded all contributed to the package that was placed before Synod. It is very hard to appreciate why the legislation is as it is without stepping back and seeing the very long journey that has brought us to this place.

What Price Unity?

Events such as the appointment to and subsequent withdrawal from the See of Sheffield of the Right Revd Philip North in spring 2017 indicate that the journey in this matter is far from over. It is too early to assess the long-term viability of the vision and, in particular, the outworking of the Five Guiding Principles. Some remain sceptical about the advisability of enacting such an approach, arguing that it makes little logical or emotional sense to try to hold together in one church both those who wholeheartedly support the ordination and consecration of women and those who do not. Others are committed to the principle but are less sure about what it means in practice. Others still consider the Five Guiding Principles to be the only realistic way forward if we are to remain faithful to the vision of a Church of England as a place that can hold together a wide range of views, on this or other matters.

My own view is that, theologically, we are required to try to hold together. The witness of the New Testament texts is to an early Church that experienced wide diversity and that, nevertheless, sought to maintain the vision of unity in the body of Christ. Diversity is not new. Nor is the uphill struggle to maintain unity in the face of that diversity. Nevertheless, the call to unity remained then and remains now. Living together with people whose views, backgrounds and traditions are different from our own has always been and will always be painful. The real mistake we make is the assumption that once something becomes 'the norm' it no longer costs. The reality is that the decision to attempt to walk the path of faith together with those who do not agree with us is sacrificial and no easy task. It is always a mistake to assume that once a decision is made, the cost of that decision disappears. The cost goes on for all concerned, and we do well to pay attention to that cost.

Allied to this, the decision to attempt to trudge the hard path of living together with those with whom we disagree does need revisiting on a regular basis. Not with the intention of unpicking the decision but with the intention of evaluating what we are learning along the way. Where are the pinch points? What have we learnt from each other? Where are the walls still firmly and thoroughly in place? Where could we live together more thoroughly if only we had the chance? It seems to me that one of the challenges of the Five Guiding Principles is that they are just that, principles. What is not happening, and what needs to happen, is the paying of careful, methodical and pastoral attention to the practical out-workings of those principles, ensuring that where they are required in practice the full ramifications of what they mean are understood and work is put in place to address the concerns they raise.[11]

It seems to me that this is a piece of learning that is urgent and pressing. Holding together the diversity of views held by the varying members of the Church of England will only get more and more challenging as time goes on. We need to learn lessons that will equip us to face the even greater challenges of the future. Living well with diversity is a vital way in which we bear witness, in our conflict-riven world, to the God who created the world in harmony and looks forward to the time when the new heaven and new earth will, at last, be at one. It is how we live out Jesus' own prayer that 'they may all be one . . . so that the world may believe that you sent me' (John 17.21). It is not easy but it is a radical and essential part of our calling as Christians.

Conclusions

The journey towards the consecration of women as bishops has changed the Church of England for ever. Some of the ways in which this has happened are huge, not least the fact that we now have bishops who are women both in the House and in the College of

---

11 It is also important to continue the theological and ecclesiological conversations begun when the legislation was being drawn up. Many conversations that took place around the Sheffield appointment in spring 2017 revealed that many people were not aware that extensive theological exploration had already taken place in the process of drawing up the legislation. Effective communication of what is already in place, alongside additional further reflection in years to come around the lived consequences of the decision made, will be essential.

Bishops; other changes are much smaller, for example the tendency to talk about the three orders of ministry in terms of what makes them unique. Some of the changes have happened, some are being lived out now and others still will only become clear in the future.

Nevertheless we need to acknowledge that the journey towards the consecration of women as bishops has had a greater impact on the life and ecclesiology of the Church of England than 'simply' the consecration of women. Those of us who love the Church of England would do well to reflect in depth on the nature of this impact, asking what needs further thought and correction, what needs acceptance and celebration and, most importantly of all, what lessons we need to learn from it that can and should be applied to other issues that we now face in the Church.

Journeys change us – that is a natural part of living. The wise traveller is one who can identify the nature and impact of the change so that, as we journey on, we journey with greater and deeper wisdom.

9

Michael Perham in the Narrative of Women in the Church

CHRISTINA REES CBE

I am writing this essay a few days before the funeral of the Revd Dr Una Kroll. It was Una who in 1978, following the failure to pass a vote in General Synod that would have opened the orders of deacon, priest and bishop to women, shouted from the visitors' gallery in Church House, 'We asked you for bread and you gave us a stone!'

At that time, Michael Perham would have been in his first post as curate of St Mary's Church, Addington, in the Diocese of Canterbury. Eleven years later, in 1989, he became a member of General Synod, which was once again preparing to debate women's ordination. In 1985, Synod had passed a vote allowing women to become deacons and in 1992 the vote opening the priesthood to women was passed. Two years later 1,500 women deacons, many of whom had been ministering in the Church for decades as deaconesses, and before that, parish workers, were ordained as priests. It would be another twenty years, however, before the vote permitting women to be bishops was passed by General Synod. During that time, Michael became an increasingly strong and out-spoken advocate for women, not only by taking part in debates in General Synod, but also by working in a variety of ways to ensure that the women bishops' legislation was passed.

I first met Michael Perham when I was elected onto General Synod in 1990, a year after he had become a member and while he was Team Rector of Oakdale in Poole. The issue of ordaining women as priests dominated synod agendas, conversations in cor-ridors and the reporting of the Church in the media. Having been one of the spokespersons in favour of women's ordination in the

Diocese of St Albans, very quickly I became an unofficial spokes-person for the campaign nationally. In the spring of 1992, with only a few months until the decisive vote on women priests, I was asked by the Movement for the Ordination of Women to assist with their strategy and publicity in the run-up to the vote.

After the first ordinations of women as priests, while Michael was still Dean of Derby, he invited me to speak on the subject of women bishops in Derby Cathedral. It was then I met Michael's wife Alison and, I believe, at least one or two of their four daugh-ters! It was vital to have the continuity of support from those who, like Michael, were not only in favour of having women as priests but who were equally committed to making it possible for women to become bishops.

'Making it possible' turned out to be the work of two decades and involved the contributions of hundreds and thousands of people inside and outside the church of England. Michael's knowl-edge of church structures and systems, his theological understand-ing and his savvy political instincts became invaluable.

If the vote in 1978 had been passed, there would have been no further need of campaigning. The matter of women's ordination as deacons, priests and bishops would have been settled at one time. That's what the Anglican Church in Sudan managed to do in their synod debate in 2000.[1] As it was, soon after the 1978 vote fell, the Movement for the Ordination of Women (MOW) was formed with the specific objective of opening the priest-hood to women. Those involved decided MOW should become a single-issue campaign group. True to their original intention, in the summer of 1994, after the first ordinations of all the wait-ing deacons had taken place, MOW held a wonderful party and folded – mission accomplished.

For the next two years, there was no national group that picked up where MOW had left off. In London, those who had been working hard for women to be allowed to become priests started up London WATCH – Women and the Church – recognizing that

1 *Women Bishops in the Church of England: A Report of the House of Bishops' Working Party on Women in the Episcopate* (London: Church House Publishing, 2004), p. 279.

the work for women's full inclusion in the ordained ministries of the Church of England must continue. It was not until November 1996 that National WATCH was formed, with ten wide-ranging objectives designed to bring about an end to all discrimination against women in the Church. It became apparent very quickly that until and unless women could be bishops, all the other objectives would be long in coming. Little did we imagine that the primary focus of working towards making it possible for women to be bishops was to shape WATCH's strategy for nearly the next twenty years.

In a very real sense the campaign had to be fought all over again. In Anglican ecclesiology, the different orders do not signify a different understanding of ordination between priests and bishops. Bishops are appointed from priests, and priests from deacons; indeed bishops are ordained as both deacons and priests before their consecration as bishop. (Of course, ordained ministers also remain part of the laos, the people of God.) It is not as if bishops are chosen from a different species, as some of the objections to ordaining women seemed to imply.

There was, however, throughout the entire campaign a strong sense of the disease that some people felt at the thought of consecrating women as bishops, in spite of being able to experience the ministry of women as priests. This pointed up the strange and more general disconnect between relating to women as mothers, sisters, wives, daughters, aunts, cousins, colleagues, bosses, friends and, increasingly, priests, and the thought of having women as bishops. Some people simply could not – or would not – see that female bishops would be just women, in the way that male bishops were just men. From the range and strength of the fears expressed, it became clear that some people could not integrate their thoughts about the women they knew and their attitudes towards women being consecrated as bishops.

This disconnect was often revealed in startling ways. It is well documented that women deacons wearing their clerical collars, and later, after the first ordinations of women as priests, women were variously told that they were 'witches and should be burned at the stake', and that some men would 'rather ordain a pork pie' or a cat. Perhaps most infamously, around the time of the vote for women priests, Dr Graham Leonard, the then Bishop of London, stated that having women as priests would be 'a virus in the bloodstream of the Church that could never be got out'.

As the late Monica Furlong pointed out in her devastating book, *A Dangerous Delight*,[2] tracing the history of the churches' attitudes towards women, this chilling phrase, uttered at a time when AIDS was just beginning to appear in the public consciousness, showed how some people equated ordained women with introducing a toxic influence in an otherwise holy, pure and vibrant body.

The Act of Synod

These attitudes were exemplified most starkly in the Church by an Act that was passed in General Synod almost one year to the day after the vote for women to be ordained as priests, well before the campaign for women bishops got under way.

The Episcopal Ministry Act of Synod, or Act of Synod, as it became known, created a precedence that not only undermined the understanding and unity of episcopacy in the Church of England, but that also revealed the toxic attitudes towards women that Monica Furlong had identified.

In the months leading up to the vote for women as priests, various arrangements had been discussed for accommodating the clergy and laity who did not accept women's ordination. The legislation contained two resolutions that parishes could pass, allowing them to refuse to appoint a female incumbent, or to refuse to have a visiting woman priest take services. The arrangements also contained financial provisions for any priests who felt unable to continue ministering in a church that ordained women. Over the ten years in which men were allowed to resign, over £27 million was reportedly paid out to around 500 priests, some of whom later returned to active, stipendiary ministry in the Church of England.

---

2 Monica Furlong, *A Dangerous Delight: Women and Power in the Church* (London: SPCK, 1991).

At one of the bishops' meetings after the decisive vote for women's ordination to the priesthood, the Act was agreed as the best way to proceed for those who remained opposed. Although the women priests' legislation had taken many years – all the time since the narrow defeat in 1978 of the legislation opening all three orders to women – the Act was pulled together within months of the vote in November 1992. Instead of sending the draft proposals for the Act to every diocese for debate and voting, as had been done with the women priests' legislation, the Act was brought in its final form to General Synod in November 1993. It was passed overwhelmingly, with hardly more than a dozen brave members voting against it.

There had, of course, been many discussions in MOW about whether or not to come out definitively for or against the Act of Synod. In the end, it was decided to advise members of General Synod to vote as they deemed best, pointing out the pros and cons of the Act.

During the debate, Dr John Habgood, the then Archbishop of York, and others, were passionate in their support of the Act, presenting it as the only proper response for those who remained opposed to women's priestly ministry and asking Synod to trust the bishops to ensure fair play for women clergy. Swayed by the insistence that the Act was the only generous Christian response, I voted for the Act. In twenty-five years as a member of General Synod, having voted in hundreds, if not thousands, of debates, it is the only vote I regret.

While recognizing that for some clergy and laity in the Church, the Act created a space where they could feel safe, the negative consequences of passing the Act of Synod soon became apparent. Resolution C, contained in the Act, created a separate strand of up to three bishops, specially consecrated men who opposed ordaining women, to be known as Provincial Episcopal Visitors (PEVs). These were almost immediately dubbed 'flying bishops' and cartoons appeared in the press of frocked and mitred men winging their way across a divided church. The reality was that while the vast majority of church members welcomed women priests, those against were vocal in their continued opposition.

In 2000, seven years after the passing of the Act of Synod, supporters of women's ordination created GRAS, the Group for Rescinding the Act of Synod. GRAS campaigned tirelessly, but were never to see the rescinding of the Act. Eventually, though, it was dismantled as part of the eventual women bishops' legislation. GRAS had a final meeting and, like MOW much earlier, it closed.

At about the same time as GRAS came into being, a review of the Act was initiated by Synod, chaired by the then Bishop of Blackburn. In spite of hundreds of critical submissions, it failed to grasp the significance and implications of the Act and amounted to little more than a whitewash. Also at this time, Helen Thorne, a PhD student in Bristol University, was writing her doctorate on the first 1,500 women to have been ordained as priests. In her thesis, she denounced the Act of Synod as being 'deeply harmful to women on a practical, emotional and spiritual level', and concluded that the Act fostered a 'theology of "taint" whereby a man's ministry is made void through his association with a woman priest'.[3] Even Anthony Howard, writing about the Act of Synod in *The Times*, commented that 'in appeasing prejudice', the Act 'legitimised it', and observed drily that there 'could hardly have been a worse example of weedy Anglican compromise'.[4]

Some of the impetus for GRAS came from Monica Furlong's collection of essays in a book called *Act of Synod, Act of Folly?*, published in 1998. In her contribution to the book, the Revd Dr Judith Maltby, Chaplain and Fellow of Corpus Christi College, Oxford, forensically examined the theology of the Act, revealing, among other things, the fourth-century Donatist heresy it inadvertently revived. Much later, Article 26 of the Thirty-Nine

---

3 Helen Thorne, *Journey to Priesthood*, CCSRG Monograph Series 3 (Bristol: Department of Theology and Religious Studies, University of Bristol, 2000).

4 *The Times*, 20 November 2001, quoted in Voices of This Calling, ed. Christina Rees (Norwich: Canterbury Press, 2002).

Articles[5] would underscore the rejection of the Donatist heresy by stating that the individual qualities of a validly ordained minister do not affect the authenticity and worthiness of the sacraments administered by that person.

In examining this 'theology of taint' implicit in the Act, Maltby also observed that 'Your bishop can deny the resurrection, the Trinity, and the incarnation; he may be a racist, liar or thief – but no one will offer you a PEV. But if he ordains a woman to the priesthood, you can call in a "safe pair of hands".'[6]

If this sounds like ancient history, fast forward to late 2016, two years after the women bishops' legislation had passed. In November, a church in Fulham urged its members to pass a new resolution under arrangements called the London Plan, explaining that by passing the resolution they 'would ensure (the vicar's) successor would be male'. It is difficult to calculate the damage done to the integrity of the episcopate and, of course, to women, over the years since the passing of the Act.

+++

After the Movement for the Ordination of Women decided to close in 1994, MOW's Secretary, Jenny Standage, continued to receive

---

5 OF THE UNWORTHINESS OF THE MINISTERS, WHICH HINDERS NOT THE EFFECT OF THE SACRAMENT although in the visible Church the evil be ever mingled with the good, and sometimes the evil have chief authority in the Ministration of the Word and Sacraments, yet forasmuch as they do not the same in their own name, but in Christ's, and do minister by his commission and authority, we may use their Ministry, both in hearing the Word of God, and in receiving of the Sacraments. Neither is the effect of Christ's ordinance taken away by their wickedness, nor the grace of God's gifts diminished from such as by faith and rightly do receive the Sacraments ministered unto them; which be effectual, because of Christ's institution and promise, although they be ministered by evil men. Nevertheless, it appertaineth to the discipline of the Church, that inquiry be made of evil Ministers, and that they be accused by those that have knowledge of their offences; and finally being found guilty, by just judgement be deposed.

6 Judith Maltby, 'One Lord, One Faith, One Baptism, but Two Integrities', in *Act of Synod, Act of Folly?*, ed. Monica Furlong (Norwich: SCM Press, 1998), p. 56.

non-stop requests from schools and universities for information about the situation of women in the Church. As the most recent MOW spokesperson, I continued to receive numerous requests from the press and media for interviews on radio and television, requests to speak, and for articles on the present and future state of ordained women. There was a deep interest in the first women priests and about how well the Church was integrating them into its systems and structures. Of course, there were questions about what opposition the women still faced – journalists wanting to be told the inevitable horror stories.

Had some women clergy really been asked when interviewing for a new post whether they had sex on Saturday nights? Had some of them been quizzed on whether they would celebrate communion when menstruating? Were younger women asked about the possibility of their becoming pregnant? Were women clergy routinely asked about their childcare arrangements when male clergy were not? The inelegant teething pains of widening the ordained priesthood to include women revealed a church filled with everything from joyful and wholehearted acceptance of women priests, to ambivalence, even to bitterly warped and misogynistic attitudes towards all women, not just ordained women. Ordaining women as priests had uncovered what Monica Furlong called a deep 'malaise' about women at the heart of society.

It was perhaps these often unspoken – and often denied – attitudes towards women that were most difficult to address. It is one thing to present a logical rationale for why certain assurances should or should not be written into legislation, but to encounter unrecognized, unconscious prejudice was to have to navigate treacherous waters while on a continually pitching and rolling deck. Even some of the 'good guys', the more supportive male laity and clergy, could expose attitudes that revealed subconscious inconsistency, at the very least, towards women. In what was not an isolated incident, after women had been priests for several years, a bishop who had been a staunch supporter learned of two clergywomen in his diocese who were at loggerheads and commented: 'We ordain women and this is what we get!' One can only assume he had never encountered friction or disagreement between two of his male clergy.

+++

In spite of these incidents and the battles over the serious implications of the Act of Synod, and the ongoing opposition of some in the Church, the years following the ordination of women to the priesthood were filled with much joy and celebration. As women began discovering the expected – and unexpected – delights, depths, demands and new dimensions of ministering as priests, their congregations also found themselves discovering ways in which having women in priestly sacramental, pastoral and practical roles challenged and changed their views of the priesthood, of women and of God. A typical reaction would be for a long-standing member of the congregation suddenly to realize, for instance, that their experience of eucharistic worship had changed, or that their understanding of the nature of God had been transformed.

From its inception in 1996, in addition to all its work responding to requests for information from schools and universities, and for interviews on radio and television, WATCH began to work on the best way forward for formally introducing the subject of women bishops onto the agenda of General Synod.

In 2000, after many months of private discussions, the then Archdeacon of Rochester, the Venerable Judith Rose, submitted a motion asking the House of Bishops to 'initiate further study on the episcopate, focusing on the issues that need to be addressed in preparation for the debate on women in the episcopate in the Church of England'. The motion was passed and the House of Bishops Working Party on Women in the Episcopate was established – commonly known as the Rochester Commission. Four years later the Commission produced a report that was debated by General Synod in 2005.

Later that year General Synod voted to start removing the legal obstacles to having women as bishops. Michael Perham, then Bishop of Gloucester, and Christopher Hill, then Bishop of Guildford, were asked to start the process. Within a year, they had consulted with a large number of groups and individuals and produced a report. I remember meeting with the bishops with a delegation from WATCH, and seeing the group from Forward in Faith waiting to follow us in to make their submission, some of whom had become friends, in spite of our differences of opinion about ordaining women. Talking to Michael privately at that time I sensed both his determination to complete the report within the timeframe, and the immense pressure he was under to do so.

The Guildford and Gloucester Report was published early in 2006. Later that year when the General Synod debated the report, it passed the recommendation that having women as bishops is 'consonant with the faith of the Church as the Church has received it'. A legislative drafting group was set up to prepare the draft measure and the amending canon that would also be necessary to remove the legislation that at that time explicitly prohibited women from becoming bishops.

It took years of drafting, debating, setting up Steering and Revision Committees, and all the many other stages and elements that go into preparing for passing major legislation in the Church of England. Across the road from Church House, the Houses of Parliament were becoming increasingly impatient with the length of time it was taking the Church to reach the point of sending the women bishops measure to them for final ratifying. For many people in the Church, lay and ordained, including bishops, the protracted journey between allowing women to become priests and allowing them to become bishops was eroding their confidence in the Church overall to respond to what they believed was the leading of the Holy Spirit.

+++

On 28 June 2012, Michael Perham gave a Presidential Address to the Gloucester Diocesan Synod. Among other issues, he commented on the process of the Church moving towards opening the episcopate to women. By that time, 42 out of the 44 dioceses of the Church of England had given approval to the measure that would make it possible for women to be bishops. Before bringing the measure to General Synod for final approval, however, the House of Bishops had exercised its right to amend the legislation. One of the two amendments the House proposed was considered to be uncontroversial. The other was to add a clause designed to enable those opposed to women becoming bishops to feel they could vote for the overall measure. This clause, 5(1)(c), was to write into the actual legislation the arrangement that had been proposed to be placed in a separate code of practice, which would not have the same legal force. It concerned the arrangements for parishes to be able to request the ministry of a male priest or bishop who shared their theological objections to women. The proposed amendment was a step too far and there was a powerfully negative reaction not only from women clergy but from many others, lay and ordained.

Michael wanted to communicate to his diocesan synod that he had not been in favour of the amendment. He told them, 'Episcopal collegiality and confidentiality prevents me from sharing with you what my advice to the House was on this matter, though some of you might guess,' and he went on to acknowledge the outpouring of 'anger, hurt and dismay among many who want to see women admitted to the episcopate'.

After explaining the significance of the amendment, and observing that many more people than the bishops had expected were deeply opposed to including Clause 5(1)(c), Michael commented that in his view 'this is partly for a broad reason that the amending of the legislation is experienced by women clergy as yet another failure to affirm the ministry of women, another instance of looking at it as if women clergy are a problem, rather than a wonderful God-given gift to the Church'.

He mentioned that eighteen of the most senior women clergy in the Church had written a letter to all members of General Synod saying they were now unable to support the measure. So problematic was the specific clause that the women had decided they would rather vote against the entire women bishops' legislation than vote for it with the clause included, and expressed their hope that General Synod would adjourn the debate scheduled to take place in July and return the legislation to the House of Bishops 'for further reflection'. Michael stated that this was also his view, although he realized that an adjournment would mean yet more delay until the vote for final approval. In his opinion, it was a price worth paying in order to avoid a 'debacle' that he believed would be a 'catastrophe for the Church of England'. In the event, General Synod voted overwhelmingly to adjourn the debate, giving the House of Bishops time to agree to remove the offending clause. Although that particular 'catastrophe' had been averted, when the General Synod next met, an even more dramatic event was to happen.

On 20 November 2012, the draft legislation for women bishops was debated, with the widespread assumption that it would pass. It gained the required two-thirds majorities in the Houses of Bishops and Clergy but fell in the House of Laity – by just six votes. The wider Church and the nation were shocked, confused and enraged. After all, several years earlier, 42 of the 44 dioceses had voted to proceed to opening the episcopate to women. How could this have happened?

The crash and burn of the women bishops' legislation in November 2012 initially had a devastating effect: some clergy and lay people commenting that they would leave the Church. There were widespread outpourings of grief and a sense of having been betrayed by General Synod. Very quickly, however, the failed vote began to galvanize people. That meeting of General Synod coincided with the retirement of Dr Rowan Williams, the then Archbishop of Canterbury. His successor, Justin Welby, was determined to find a way to turn around the defeat and instigated plans for facilitated conversations for the next synods. Within a year and a half, the legislation and accompanying guidelines had been redrafted, and on 14 July 2014 the women bishops measure was passed.

Those last few meetings of General Synod were times of high pressure. For some years, Michael Perham had been coming to the fringe meetings of GS WATCH, attended by members of WATCH who were also on General Synod, as well as other supporters of women bishops. Mary Johnston, of London Diocese, chaired the meetings and Hugh Lee, from Oxford Diocese, undertook all the organizing. In the eighteen months between the failure of the women bishops' legislation in November 2012, and the successful passing of the eventual women bishops measure in July 2014, Michael started coming to various other meetings of supporters called during synod, some meeting in private homes near Church House, when synod sessions were held in London, and others held in rooms at the University of York, for the remaining July sessions.

Michael began to take a leading role in these meetings, pulling them together and encouraging people to attend. When in York, the formal sessions of General Synod do not finish until 10pm, and so it was usually around 10.30pm, after a long and arduous day of debating, that a group of between twelve and twenty members would meet in a room on the first floor of one of the colleges. Michael chaired these informal meetings, working on strategies for the debates, usually taking place the next day. He would ensure that we covered all possible angles of the debate and then identify those who were most able to speak on the various topics.

Even though I was invariably exhausted during these meetings, as was everyone else, I remember a sense of excitement, focus and determination. As specific areas to address in the debate were identified, people would volunteer to cover them in their speeches. Sometimes several people were lined up to take on certain points. It was impossible, of course, to know who would be called to speak, so there had to be backups if any one of us wasn't chosen.

Michael was extremely efficient and kept us focused in spite of our fatigue, doing so with a light touch and a minimum of extraneous discussion, as it was important that we had time to write our speeches, and time to sleep! Some nights we were so tired we were almost punch drunk, and there was laughter as well as serious conversation.

It is impossible to write adequately here about the long journey towards having women as priests and bishops in the Church of England. Nor is it possible to include a comprehensive summary of Michael's contributions to that journey. I can only hope this brief essay expresses even a tiny part of the intensity, complexity and passion of the many years of campaigning. Michael's involvement was valuable and significant and I offer to him these words with my gratitude and love.

Good News for All

NICHOLAS HOLTAM

Michael Perham preached his last sermon in Salisbury Cathedral on Ash Wednesday. It was understated and astonishing, launching the diocese in Praying Together with about 25,000 of us committed to doing just that through Lent. In the previous fortnight he had run four workshops on prayer for over 500 people. To get ready for the early evening service to mark the beginning of Lent, he had slept for fourteen hours the night before and for two hours during the day. He sat in the sanctuary throughout and preached from a chair placed centrally from which he read his sermon, not trusting his mind to be able to deliver something more spontaneous from notes. Yet he made it look effortless. The manner of his delivery conveyed the message. He quoted George Herbert, priest and poet who served in Bemerton just outside Salisbury, and welcomed the feast of Lent. He spoke of our accepting the disciplines of self-examination and repentance, prayer, fasting and self-denial, of reading and meditating on God's holy word, and of our accepting the cross being laid on us with joy.

We prayed together, cathedral and diocese. Michael's strong sense of our being together as the Church in the way of Jesus Christ is fundamental to the life of a bishop. In the Church, disciples who do not see, think and do the same as each other belong together 'in Christ'. This is not novel. We read it in the Scriptures as the disciples are called again into a community of the resurrection and the early Church tested the meaning and significance of difference within a fundamental unity. It means difference and change has to be negotiated, sometimes formally through the synods and councils of the Church, sometimes informally and locally as people seek to live by faith and try new things in new circumstances in good conscience, faithfully seeing whether something is of God and takes root in our shared life in the life of the Church.

One of my own responsibilities as a bishop is for ministry with and among deaf and disabled people. Within the Church, there is a desire to include people who are deaf and disabled. They have different needs that sometimes raise difficult questions about whether they and their contribution are really welcome. The accessibility of buildings and adaptation of language and practice give signals about whether we are really interested in inclusion and in our praying and being together.

The issue of who is included is, and always has been, a hot topic in the life of the Church. In the early Church, could Gentiles become Christian without also keeping Jewish Law in relation to food and circumcision? It is striking that this bitter debate about the inclusion of the Gentiles in the Epistle to the Galatians gets broadened by Paul to include other key divisions in ancient society not actually dealt with directly in the Epistle. The Christian gospel is good news for all who are willing to receive it and be baptized into the life of Christ.

> As many of you as were baptized into Christ have clothed your-selves with Christ. There is no longer Jew or Greek, there is no longer slave or free, there is no longer male and female; for all of you are one in Christ Jesus. And if you belong to Christ, then you are Abraham's offspring, heirs according to the promise. (Galatians 3.27–29)

General Synod and Same-Sex Relationships

Ash Wednesday with the launch of Praying Together took place two weeks after the Church of England's General Synod debated the 'Report from the House of Bishops on Marriage and Same Sex Relationships after the Shared Conversations'.[1] In what was

---

1 *Church of England Report from the House of Bishops on Marriage and Same Sex Relationships after the Shared Conversations* (2017), GS 2055.

a passionate and good-natured debate, by a small majority in the House of Clergy but also with a large minority in the House of Laity, Synod decided not to 'take note' of the report.[2] It was a report that was thought not to be good news for all.

Despite our having the same range of views as the wider Church, though probably in different proportions, the House of Bishops was unanimous in support of this report.[3] It offered an agreed way forward. The report was explicit about our disagreements and noted that

> Anglicanism has always been a contested tradition. Our vocation to be the spiritual home for all the people of England has, historically, enabled us to work together despite the distinctives of catholic, evangelical, and liberal traditions.[4]

The report also noted that the discussion of same-sex relationships arose well before *Issues in Human Sexuality*[5] was published in 1991 but it did not give the history of this. That was probably sensible given the extent of it, but it might have been helpful to recall the Church of England's contributions in the 1950s and 60s to the decriminalization of homosexual acts by consenting adults in private. At the time this was deeply contentious. It took ten years before recommendations from the Wolfenden Report became part of the Sexual Offences Act in 1967. In this discussion, by careful listening to those most closely involved and by reason and engagement with the Christian tradition, the Church

---

2 The overall vote was 242 in favour of taking note and 184 against but there had to be a majority in each House, or category of membership: House of Bishops 43 for, 1 against; House of Clergy 93 in favour, 100 against, 2 abstentions; House of Laity 106 in favour, 83 against, 4 abstentions. Hence General Synod did not take not of the Report.

3 The Bishop of Coventry inadvertently voted against and apologized afterwards.

4 *Report on Marriage and Same Sex Relationship*, para 8.

5 *Issues in Human Sexuality: A Statement by the House of Bishops of the General Synod of the Church of England*, December 1991.

of England gave significant moral leadership and service to Church and nation.[6]

A markedly different style was adopted in 1987 when, after a heated debate in which a private member's motion was significantly modified, the General Synod voted by 403 votes to 8 that

This Synod affirms that the biblical and traditional teaching on chastity and fidelity in personal relationships is a response to, and expression of, God's love for each one of us, and in particular affirms:

1. that sexual intercourse is an act of total commitment which belongs properly within a permanent married relationship;
2. that fornication and adultery are sins against this ideal, and are to be met by a call to repentance and the exercise of compassion;
3. that homosexual genital acts also fall short of this ideal, and are likewise to be met by a call to repentance and the exercise of compassion;
4. that all Christians are called to be exemplary in all spheres of morality, including sexual morality; and that holiness of life is particularly required of Christian leaders.

Here Synod took a clear stand. It was presented as 'a Biblical witness to our nation' but one effect of it has been thirty years of ecclesiastical introspection about matters of sexuality. In 1991 it led on to the House of Bishops making a statement, 'Issues in Human Sexuality'.[7] This was intended for education and debate but its use solidified almost into law. It has informed practice particularly in relation to ordained ministry in the years since. The Church has looked increasingly out of touch with a rapidly changing culture, only capable of asserting truths and unable to comment in an engaged way that would help society negotiate

---

6 *Report of the Departmental Committee on Homosexual Offences and Prostitution*, 1957, known as the Wolfenden Report after the committee's chairman, Lord Wolfenden. The Committee included a significant number of Anglicans and the Church contributed greatly to the ensuing discussion that shaped the eventual legislation.

7 *Issues in Human Sexuality*, 1991.

profound change in human self-understanding and relationships. A significant number of people, particularly young people, now think the Church's inability to adapt in relation to issues of gender and sexual orientation make us less than moral, 'a toxic brand'.

Michael Perham was a member of the working group chaired by Sir Joseph Pilling on human sexuality,[8] which reported in 2013. They recognized the range of divergent views in the Church about homosexuality and proposed two years of 'facilitated conversations' to enable us to understand one another better. These 'Shared Conversations' were intended to assist careful listening, support a clear and open exchange of views and embody the principle of disagreeing Christianly, in a manner marked by Christian care for each other.[9]

The bishops were charged to respond to these Shared Conversations. In our discussions a number of principles got established among the bishops. First, there was little support for changing the Church of England's teaching on marriage despite the change in civil law that had enabled same-sex couples to marry.

Second, there was a strong sense that existing resources, guidance and tone needed to be revisited.[10] As a consequence, there was a clear (although not unanimous) weight of opinion in favour of the option framed in terms of interpreting the existing law and guidance to permit maximum freedom within it, without changes to the law or the doctrine of the Church.[11] In practice this meant:

a. establishing a fresh tone and culture of welcome and support for lesbian and gay people;
b. proposing a substantial new Teaching Document on marriage and relationships;
c. developing guidance for clergy about appropriate pastoral provision for same-sex couples;

---

8 *Report of the House of Bishops Working Group on Human Sexuality* (London: Church House Publishing, 2013).

9 *Report on Marriage and Same Sex Relationships*, para 13.

10 *Report on Marriage and Same Sex Relationships*, para 18.

11 *Report on Marriage and Same Sex Relationships*, para 22.

and

d. preparing new guidance on the nature of questions put to ordinands and clergy about their lifestyle.[12]

In a prescient paragraph the report said that

Agreeing these elements would not by any means answer every pressing question for the Church of England in the area of marriage, relationships and sexuality. The hope would be, however, that they can shape a framework for the Church's continuing process of prayer, reflection and teaching within and beyond the General Synod, helping to focus it constructively on specific areas.[13]

In all of this the bishops were trying to shape what might happen next after the Shared Conversations. For Synod not to take note is very unusual. It was clear that a substantial minority of Synod thought the bishops had not summarized the current position of the Church accurately or proposed for the future helpfully. Some might also have felt excluded in a process that had until then been involving but was now directive with only the opportunity to take note, or not. A great deal of what was said in the debate was said personally and movingly. It was striking that LGBTI people had found their confidence to speak openly and in my opinion the centre of gravity in Synod moved.

Three big issues recurred and need attention.

A Change of Tone

The report acknowledged that a change of tone is needed which is affirming and welcoming of LGBTI people. In this the report was significantly different from what had gone before but in Synod

---

12 *Report on Marriage and Same Sex Relationships*, para 23.
13 *Report on Marriage and Same Sex Relationships*, para 27.

and in the wider debate people kept saying the bishops had broken trust with people who had made themselves vulnerable in the Shared Conversations. In part this was about the bishops not delivering the change that some now expect but above all what was wrong was that LGBTI people were still being talked about as if they were out there rather than already in the Church. Speaker after speaker said, 'We are here and we are not going away.' The attempted change in tone was undermined by the failure to talk about 'us' rather than 'them'.

The Archbishop of Canterbury addressed this directly at the end of the debate and in his statement afterwards when he said:

> No person is a problem, or an issue. People are made in the image of God. All of us, without exception, are loved and called in Christ. There are no 'problems', there are simply people.[14]

There does seem to be a desire to change the tone. In recent years homophobia has been condemned by all sides of this debate. The Primates of the Anglican Communion have made a creditable stand against the criminalization of homosexuality. There was a genuine attempt to change the tone in the bishops' report even though what came across was that we bishops just don't get it.

What we know from other change processes is that unless the people being talked about are in the room, those in power retain control and the conversation does not change enough. In South Africa, for example, apartheid changed when non-white people were included in the informal and formal conversation with the people who held the institutional power. That happened in the Shared Conversations, which must be why there was a sense of betrayal by the bishops when it came to this report. There is only one openly gay bishop in a civil partnership and as a suffragan bishop he is a member of the College of Bishops but not the House of Bishops. Nor was he appointed to be one of the ten who were the Bishops' Reflection Group on this issue. It is now evident that the absence of openly LGBTI people in the conversations

---

14 Archbishop of Canterbury, *Statement following today's General Synod*, Wednesday 15 February 2017.

is damaging the outcomes of the process. One outcome of the debate is that 'Don't talk about us without us' has been heard and accepted.

The Archbishop of Canterbury's statement following the Synod debate went in this direction in saying, 'We need to work together – not just the bishops but the whole Church, not excluding anyone – to move forward with confidence.' A letter the following day from him and the Archbishop of York, which sketched the agenda for the next phase, included

> establishing a Pastoral Oversight group led by the Bishop of Newcastle, with the task of supporting and advising Dioceses on pastoral actions with regard to our current pastoral approach to human sexuality. The group will be inclusive, and will seek to discern the development of pastoral practices, within current arrangements.[15]

Scripture

A small number of those who voted not to take note of the report hold a conservative view of Scripture and think that even to have the debate about same-sex relationships means that the Church is not taking the Bible seriously. For them the underlying issue is of faithfulness to God's Word and the expression of our sexuality is a 'first order' issue in relation to a person's salvation. Their assumption is that there is only one way to read Scripture right and the expression of love in same-sex relationships is plainly wrong and sinful. The pastoral task in relation to homosexuals is to love the sinner but hate the sin. The only options for people who are 'same-sex attracted' is celibacy or healing.

The scriptural ground has been well travelled. It may need repeating but it is unlikely to produce different conclusions. There is a huge supporting literature. All the reports on sexuality

---

15 Letter from the Archbishops of Canterbury and York to members of General Synod, 17 February 2017.

produced by the Church of England since the 1960s have had biblical sections informing each particular, slightly shifting debate. Their conclusion is that there are faithful Christians who in good conscience read and interpret Scripture differently.[16]

Six biblical passages are cited by conservatives as specific and clear evidence that the Scriptures are against homosexual acts:

- Genesis 19, in which the destruction of Sodom and Gomorrah is attributed to divine punishment for male homosexual acts.
- Leviticus 18.22 and Leviticus 20.13, which prescribe that a man who lies with a man as with a woman has committed an abomination and both parties to the act should be put to death.
- Romans 1.26–27, which includes female and male homosexuality as examples of degrading passions and an expression of idolatry.
- 1 Corinthians 6.9–10, which lists those who will not enter the Kingdom of heaven and includes *malakos* and *arsenokoites*, translated in the New Revised Standard Version as male prostitutes and sodomites.
- 1 Timothy 1.10, which includes *arsenokoites* in a list of those for whom the law is intended, to bring the disobedient to conform to the glorious gospel of the blessed God.[17]

The interpretation of these passages falls into three broad types with different implications. First, the 'plain meaning' of these texts is said to be the denunciation of homosexual practices which are contrary to the will of God. Few take the equally plain meaning of Leviticus that the death penalty is to be imposed for homosexual practices or explain why these particular texts are selected as having absolute and universal application today while others such as the prohibition of eating shellfish in Leviticus 11.12 are conveniently set aside. The explanation is, of course, that the teaching of Jesus and other New Testament texts counter the imposition of the death penalty and the significance of Jewish food laws was

---

16 What follows is based on my article on 'Homosexuality' in *Christianity: The Complete Guide*, ed. John Bowden (London: Continuum, 2005).

17 Holtam, 'Homosexuality'.

modified in the teaching of Jesus (for example Matthew 15.10–20) and the early Church (for example Acts 11.1–18). It is said that the negative understanding of homosexual practices can be strengthened by moving beyond the six specific texts to the positive expression in what is said about human sexuality and heterosexual marriage.

Second, it may be comforting to think that the plain meaning and interpretation of the text remains constant so as to avoid being captured by the spirit of the present age, but careful analysis of the contexts and the examination of the meaning and translation of individual words allows for much less certainty than might at first sight seem evident. The story of Sodom is about a breach of hospitality. The condemnation in Paul's letter to the Romans is of homosexuality associated with idolatry and paganism. The meaning and translation of the specific Greek words in the NT passages is a great deal more complex than is apparent from the plain meaning of the words adopted in English translations. This approach requires a revision of the significance of these particular texts and there is still a great deal of debate about exactly what this means.

A third type of interpretation is concerned with how an ancient text speaks today. It begins by acknowledging that the six specific texts do not address the contemporary reality of homosexual Christians. Even when words like marriage or homosexual are used in both ancient and modern sources, the difference in cultural understandings means that we are not talking about what they were talking about. The so-called 'plain' meaning is actually only a 'surface' reading, which may in fact be a wrong reading.

The serious part of our modern concern is for people who are homosexual not by deviance from their heterosexual nature, nor by preference or choice, but because of their given identity. They seek to form stable, faithful, adult, loving sexual relationships, and as Christians they want to do so within the Church of which they are baptized members.[18]

---

18 This has been especially well stated by Jeffrey John in *Permanent, Faithful, Stable: Christian Same-Sex Marriage*, revised edition (London: Darton, Longman & Todd, 2012).

In relation to what feels a very stale and unresolved debate about the Bible, I am increasingly struck by the occasions in the Scriptures when people who knew their Bible well misunderstood its message. It does seem to be a scriptural pattern to which we religious people need to pay attention. Just three examples from Luke and Acts.

The lawyer who prompted Jesus to tell the story of the Good Samaritan (Luke 10.25–37) knew and was able to recite the Law. 'Teacher,' the lawyer said, 'what must I do to inherit eternal life?' Jesus said to him, 'What is written in the law? What do you read there?' The lawyer had no difficulty replying. He knew the Law and could answer with the commandments and, for Jews, keeping the commandments is the mark of keeping faith with God. So the lawyer summarized the Law as, 'Love God and love your neighbour as yourself.' Jesus said he was right and told him to go and do it.

Wanting to justify himself – there's a problem, none of us can justify ourselves – the lawyer asked Jesus, 'And who is my neighbour?' There were a number of possible answers in Scripture: our family, kindred, tribe; people like us, Jews; or our neighbour could be the stranger, the outsider, and that's the answer Jesus gave. Jesus told the story about a man going down from Jerusalem to Jericho who fell into the hands of robbers, who stripped him, beat him and went away, leaving him half dead. A priest and Levite passed by on the other side because they had a higher duty. If they had touched a dead body they would have spoilt their religious purity. So they passed by on the other side for a good religious reason. They had a higher duty to God. But a Samaritan was moved with pity and took care of him.

For Jews at the time of Jesus the idea of there being a good Samaritan was an oxymoron. 'Which of these three, do you think, was neighbour to the man who fell into the hands of the robbers?' asked Jesus. The lawyer couldn't even say the name, for Jews despised Samaritans. 'The one who showed him mercy,' he said. This story is discomforting to the religious by giving priority to our acting mercifully. Even worse, it was a despised outsider who showed a Jewish lawyer the true meaning of the Jewish Law.

Or what about the disciples on the road to Emmaus (Luke 24.13–32)? They were puzzled and downhearted by events in Jerusalem in which all their hopes seemed to have come to naught. They knew Jesus well but for some reason they did not recognize the 'stranger' who joined them on their journey. He came along-side, listened and then took them through the Scriptures which they surely knew but, in new circumstances, did not understand. They did not understand what we now might think of as the plain meaning of the text. It was in the breaking of bread that he was known to them in an instant and then the risen Lord was gone.

Because of the resurrection, Christianity became a missionary religion by sending the Church outwards with good news for all people. In the Acts of the Apostles 8.26–40 there is a story about the baptism of an Ethiopian eunuch. It sounds an exotic story to us and its meaning is no longer obvious but it is one of the great missionary stories of the New Testament.

An angel of the Lord said to Philip, 'Get up and go toward the south to the road that goes down from Jerusalem to Gaza'.

This is the wilderness road to Gaza, a harsh environment in which human experience is vivid and clear.

Now there was an Ethiopian eunuch, a court official of the Candace, queen of the Ethiopians, in charge of her entire treasury.

The gospel is going south, outwards from the Jewish world to Gentiles. The Ethiopian is an African, presumably a black man from the edge of the known world. In Greek the word eunuch means 'the keeper of the bed chamber'. In other words he is a safe and in himself powerless male. Such people could be trusted to look after other people's privacy, or power, or wealth, as with the Queen of Ethiopia's treasury. Throughout Mesopotamia eunuchs were given sensitive personal and political roles.

In Israel eunuchs were despised and were outcasts. Deuteronomy 23.1 could not be more graphic a piece of legislation making it clear that eunuchs shall not be admitted to the assembly of the Lord:

No one whose testicles are crushed or whose penis is cut off shall be admitted to the assembly of the LORD.

Now this eunuch was riding in his chariot down the desert road, reading from the prophet Isaiah. These were some of the verses in Isaiah 53 about the suffering servant that the early Church used so unexpectedly to identify Jesus as that sort of Messiah.

Like a sheep that is led to the slaughter,
and like a lamb silent before its shearer,
so he does not open his mouth.
In his humiliation justice was denied him.
Who can describe his generation?
For his life is taken away from the earth.

Read on and Isaiah 56 promises that after the restoration of Israel the faithful eunuchs and foreigners will be gathered to the house of the Lord: the outcast will be gathered in.

Philip ran up to the chariot and asked, 'Do you understand what you are reading?' He climbed in and, starting with the Scripture, proclaimed the good news about Jesus. When they saw water, on the wilderness road, the Ethiopian eunuch asked, 'What is to stop me from being baptized?' Nothing can stop him: faithful eunuchs and foreigners will be gathered into the house of the Lord. This is good news for all.

These three stories are not about homosexuality. They are about good religious people who know their Bible without understanding its meaning, and they are about the good news of Jesus Christ being for all people, not just for the insiders.

When I license a priest to a new ministry in the Diocese of Salisbury I ask them to 'Seek the mind of Christ'. Quite often I preach about this and say it is relatively easy to say, 'The Bible says this' or 'The Church teaches that', but what we seek is the mind of Christ here and now. To do this Anglicans use Scripture, tradition and reason in a community that worships and prays and seeks to act justly, love kindness and walk humbly with God. The six specific texts about homosexuality do not directly answer this much more important question about the mind of Christ. A richer and broader use of Scripture in this debate is capable of producing a more generous inclusive response that is good news for all and looks more like the mind of Christ.

Good Disagreement

Once upon a time I assumed that all right-thinking people would agree with me. If we looked at the facts and used our reason we would come to the same and only right answer. Long ago – was it when I was 7/8, 13/14 or 25, or am I constantly rediscovering it? – I realized that good people conscientiously disagree about important things and we are part of the rich diversity of God's creation. A Jewish friend says, 'Where there are three rabbis there are four opinions' and another replies, 'Only four?' This is true not just of Jews, it is our common human experience, but Jesus was a Jew and there is a way of being together in the Gospels that is confident about differences and of finding truth among us in community.

One of the contributions made by Justin Welby when he became Archbishop of Canterbury was his identification of the need for the Anglican Communion and Church of England in particular to rediscover 'good disagreement'. This has to include the possibility that I might be mistaken but it also has to include others within the Christian community recognizing and accepting a proper diversity to our being human and being Christian. Historically, we Christians have divided as a church over things that seem important and contradictory but more often we live with diversity and paradox in what is said to be a 'broad Church'.

One of the things we learned in the late twentieth century is the gift of human diversity and the rainbow people of God. For a period this was a gift South Africa gave the world. It is not coincidental that Archbishop Desmond Tutu is a supporter of LGBTI inclusion. He sees it as a matter of justice akin to the struggles of

South Africans in response to apartheid. For him, our relationships are governed by the justice he found in the Bible but which was fundamentally absent in the country in which he grew up. If being gay, for whatever reason, is a person's given identity rather than a lifestyle choice then it is a matter of justice they are dealt with equally.

For myself, as a vicar in the West End of London where the sexual is a very public aspect of the social, the Church was distinctly counter-cultural in persisting to proclaim the significance of faithful, lifelong, loving relationships. By focusing so much on homosexuality the Church was fixated on the wrong issue when there has been such rapid change in all people's attitudes and sexual behaviour. What gay people needed from church was acceptance and support in establishing loving, faithful, lifelong relationships. To do this needs institutional embodiment as well as effective pastoral care. The introduction of civil partnerships in 2004 was therefore a very positive step in the right direction.

At first I thought it was helpful to distinguish between same-sex civil partnerships and heterosexual marriage. Many in the churches thought the commonly used description of civil partnerships as 'gay marriage' was what philosophers call a category error. There is work to be done here. The biological relationship is clearly different but the Church's preoccupation with 'genital acts' is demeaning to a rich and fruitful life-giving relationship. The legal protection and public proclamation which civil partnership afforded gay relationships strengthened their likeness to marriage in terms of increasing commitment to working on the relationship itself, to contributing to the wellbeing of both families of origin, and to acting as responsible and open members of society. Open recognition and public support have increased in civil partnerships those very qualities of life for which marriage itself is so highly celebrated. It was not really a surprising development that civil partnerships have morphed into equal marriage, which is routinely backdated to the date of the civil partnership.

While marriage is robust and enduring, what is meant by marriage has developed and changed significantly. For example, the widespread availability of contraception from the mid-twentieth century onwards took several decades to gain acceptance for married couples by the Lambeth Conference in 1958. The newer forms of the Church of England's marriage service have since recognized that the couple *may* have children. Over the last fifty years the Church of England has come to accept that marriages intended to be lifelong can break down and that on occasion marriage after divorce can be celebrated in the context of church. It is also the case that most couples now live together before they marry. This happens without censure from the Church, which continues to conduct these marriages joyfully even though the Church's teaching is that sexual relationships are properly confined to marriage. These are examples of pastoral accommodation of very different practice even though the Church's doctrine of marriage has remained the same.

There are a variety of views within the Church of England about same-sex relationships. Although the discussion in the Church seems to be painfully slow, we are in fact experiencing rapid social change similar to that in the wider society. This is all the more complex to express because there are those who see this issue as fundamental to the structure of Christian faith. It is also complex because of the worldwide nature of the Anglican Communion in which what might be said carefully in one cultural context, for example the UK, can be deeply damaging in another, for example parts of Africa. Change and development are essential in the Church, as they are in life, and part of the genius of a missionary church is its ability to root the good news of Jesus Christ in varied cultures in every time and place. One of the difficulties now is that globalization and communication mean it is much more difficult for Christianity to develop in culturally sensitive ways.

What the bishops were proposing was a basis for providing pastoral care and prayer where the local church thought it appropriate. As with the Gamaliel principle in Acts 5.39, if it is of God it will not be possible to overturn it. For some, this careful pastoral accommodation would appear to be unchristian and unwelcome. There has been a very uncomfortable polarization of views and the notion of good disagreement is under pressure.

Next Steps

In the immediate aftermath of the February 2017 General Synod the Archbishops set out what they saw to be the next steps. There is no evident game changer, just more careful hard work to be done together across divisions, including producing a theological document capable of bearing weight so as to replace *Issues in Human Sexuality* which, it is agreed, is no longer fit for purpose and was never intended to bear the weight it has carried.[19]

Michael Perham and I did not entirely agree about equal marriage but he was disciplined about being collaborative, instinctively inclusive and thoughtful about bridging disagreements. He cared about people. His respect for Synod and his skill in making and moving Synod would have been valuable as we seek the next steps of what is undoubtedly still a journey.

It is often said that the difference between this and other contentious issues the Church has faced in the recent past is that, as yet, there is not a consensus about where we want to get to, such as became clear with the marriage of divorcees in the lifetime of their former partner or with the ordination of women to all three orders of ministry. That is to forget the levels of disagreement that were part of the earlier stages of those discussions and I think the debate about same-sex relationships is also becoming clearer.

In February 2017 and since, a consensus has begun to emerge about the gospel of Jesus Christ being experienced as good news for all. In their letter to members of Synod the Archbishops called for, 'a radical new Christian inclusion in the Church'. They said:

The way forward needs to be about love, joy and celebration of our common humanity; of our creation in the image of God, of our belonging to Christ – all of us, without exception, without exclusion.

---

19 *Issues in Human Sexuality*, 1991.

If that is meant without ambivalence, and if the Archbishops have expressed the mind of Synod, this is no longer about pastoral accommodation, but about acceptance and celebration. The Archbishops have moved us on significantly into being a church which really does want to proclaim in word and deed the good news of Jesus Christ for all.

Afterword

There are many rather formal portraits of my predecessors on the walls of Bishopscourt and Church House in Gloucester, but the portrait of Bishop Michael Perham by Lorna May Wadsworth is a joyous contrast and the very opposite of dour.

Commissioned by the Diocese of Gloucester to mark Michael's retirement, it reveals a man full of life and love. Anyone who knew Michael would instantly recognize the posture of the open hand and the understated smile. It is unsurprising that a bishop who has given the Church the gift of so much beautiful liturgy, and who appeared most fully alive when celebrating the Eucharist,

chose to be painted wearing such vestments. Here is an overseer, the pastor's pastor, with crozier in hand teaching and blessing. His face is looking both outward and slightly upward, engaging the people in the presence of God. There is a radiance to it and the colours are sharp and bright.

That vibrancy is reflected in the brushstrokes of this book's chapters, which present personal tributes to this extraordinary man. The glory of God is seen sometimes in vivid remembrance of celebration and holiness, and sometimes as it shone through the chinks and cracks of brokenness, pain and struggle.

My friendship with Michael emerged as fellow pilgrims on some important journeys in the recent life of the Church. First, through his tireless and tenacious work to see women ordained to the episcopate; and second, when we both participated in the Bishops' Working Group on Human Sexuality chaired by Sir Joseph Pilling. On both of these paths we heard, together, faithful Christians express their deep and passionately held views. There was conflict and pain, which bore witness to deep wounds in the Body of Christ; but in those same places we also encountered the resurrection hope of Jesus Christ. And amid all of this, I experienced Michael's clarity of thought, his good sense and measured words, his quiet unwavering optimism and his capacity to keep on keeping on.

In those journeys of endless discussion, positioning and prayer, I never imagined that one day I would be called to be a bishop, let alone find myself succeeding Michael in Gloucester. It is an immense privilege, and humbling, to see my name beneath his on the long list of bishops in Gloucester Cathedral, not least because it is a reminder that our very different lives are just a small part in God's great story.

As I have reflected on those portraits of bishops past, I find it especially appropriate that Wadsworth painted Michael's portrait in Eastertide. Michael's figure is presented standing in front of Tom Denny's stunning blue stained-glass windows in a side chapel at Gloucester Cathedral. The centre window portrays Thomas the Apostle in the presence of the risen Christ. The windows either side are images of praise for God's creation, inspired by Psalm 148. The depiction of Michael's almost radiant figure, framed by the wonder of life known most fully in encounter with Jesus, overflows with hope.

In the sadness of family, friends and the Church who have lost the presence, gifts and creativity of Michael, I give thanks for my own memories of him and for the pictures of him captured in the pages of this book; but I am also thankful for the Wadsworth portrait we continue to hold. Michael's outstretched hand has become, for me, one of invitation to experience Christ's fullness of life and to be blessed. Here in the bishop and his surroundings is writ large the promise of God who makes all things new.

Of course, despite all that is good in it, it remains an imperfect reminder of Michael. The very nature of a personal portrait is that the person stands alone, and yet the person painted has been shaped through life in encounters with many different people and situations. And so it is that I must mention Michael's wife, Alison. Long before I ever met her I had heard Michael speak of her with pride and gratitude. He was keen for me to meet her, which finally happened on the day of my consecration in Canterbury. Since then it has been wonderful to experience so much more of Alison's overflowing humour, her fierce passion for mercy and justice, her honest love and her commitment to living with integrity. I believe the colours of Michael's portrait would be much less striking if Alison had not been such an integral part of his story.

And yet it is deeply poignant that both Michael and Alison have experienced what it is to stand alone and know that ultimately none of us can fully enter into the deepest thoughts, emotions and experiences of another.

Beneath the surface of the blue paint depicting the Denny windows, the artist used the same gold leaf used in the writing of icon paintings. It depicts what Wadsworth describes as 'heavenly light'. Here is heaven touching earth.

As I look at that portrait the tune 'SINE NOMINE' by the Gloucestershire-born Vaughan Williams comes to mind as I recall the words

O blest communion, fellowship divine!
We feebly struggle, they in glory shine;

all are one in thee, for all are thine.
Alleluia, Alleluia!

And yet one day there will be a 'yet more glorious day'. The saints triumphant will rise in even brighter array than that of Michael's portrait. We will be with him as 'the King of Glory passes on his way', and together we will once more sing 'Alleluia'.

Thank you, Michael.

Rt Revd Rachel Treweek
Bishop of Gloucester

Index